LIFTING THE ISLAND

LIFTING THE ISLAND

selected poems

DAVID EGGLETON

Red Hen Press | *Pasadena, CA*

Book design by Mark E. Cull.

Library of Congress Cataloging-in-Publication Data

Names: Eggleton, David, author.
Title: Lifting the island: selected poems / David Eggleton.
Description: First edition. | Pasadena, CA: Red Hen Press, 2025.
Identifiers: LCCN 2024043896 (print) | LCCN 2024043897 (ebook) | ISBN
   9781636282909 (paperback) | ISBN 9781636282916 (ebook)
Subjects: LCSH: Oceania—Poetry. | LCGFT: Poetry.
Classification: LCC PR9639.3.E42 L54 2025 (print) | LCC PR9639.3.E42
   (ebook) | DDC 821/.914—dc23/eng/20241021
LC record available at https://lccn.loc.gov/2024043896
LC ebook record available at https://lccn.loc.gov/2024043897

The National Endowment for the Arts, the Los Angeles County Arts Commission, the Ahmanson Foundation, the Dwight Stuart Youth Fund, the Max Factor Family Foundation, the Pasadena Tournament of Roses Foundation, the Pasadena Arts & Culture Commission and the City of Pasadena Cultural Affairs Division, the City of Los Angeles Department of Cultural Affairs, the Audrey & Sydney Irmas Charitable Foundation, the Meta & George Rosenberg Foundation, the Albert and Elaine Borchard Foundation, the Adams Family Foundation, Amazon Literary Partnership, the Sam Francis Foundation, and the Mara W. Breech Foundation partially support Red Hen Press.

First Edition
Published by Red Hen Press
www.redhen.org

To the memory of my mother, Kalara Loloma Sitiveni.

Contents

PART ONE

LIFTING THE ISLAND

PART TWO

THE SHALLOWS

PART THREE

THE GREAT WAVE

PART FOUR
THE WHALE ROAD

PART FIVE
THE WALL

PART SIX
BEACON

LIFTING THE ISLAND

Lifting the Island

Virtuous sunlight lifts the island to prayer.
The abyss is dizzyingly blue to dive into.
Surfers are carried on the backs of waves.
Hotels rear balcony totems notched skyward.
Heat yawns with a reptile's tranced shimmer.
Dazzled clouds somersault; then roll away,
from a day flapping in an ocean breeze.

Girls in just bikinis and flip-flops,
their long hair streaming in the wind,
weave mopeds and surfboards beach-wards,
listening to iTunes, white buds in their ears,
flat out in heavy traffic, as fat men
on fatter hogs roar along with the racket
of low-flying, propeller-driven, fighter planes.

The beachcomber who once sailed seven seas,
goes from bin to bin with freestyle hands,
grave as a mandarin in abstract thought.
Ripe stink of garbage. Hot weeks of August.
He wears nothing but faded and ripped shorts,
his muscles ripple under sun-blackened skin,
his fingers toil to free mashed drink cans.

The old gods are curios, remade in the bar
as the grinning wooden handles of beer taps.
Those at the bar, heads bowed, dream of surf,
dream of white foam swept into a cold glass.
Fleeting moments woven like flower garlands,
a seaweed hula undulating in a ship's wake.
The howl of air-con strains to cool down rooms.

Catch the smoking wave on winged heels,
orchidaceous comber that lifts rose-gold,
before deep green, light green, greener, bluer,
deeper, darker, roller-slider rising, standing,
before weight of water beneath the standing
wave topples to wipe out, because the sea
has been stopped by land shelving beneath.

Flying In, Southside

At Māngere, the airport welcomes you to Middle Earth,
coasting on a jet's wing and a karakia,
but the industrial parkland unfolds as generic,
though 'nesian mystics harmonise snatches of melody
on Bader Drive by the fale-style churches of Little Tonga,
all the way round the Town Centre to busy Pak'NSave,
from whose carpark the Mountain looks back, submerging.

Manaia sail across blue heaven to catch day-dreams;
they glide like slo-mo fa'afafine above South Auckland:
the big box stores, all in orange green yellow or red,
as big as aircraft hangars in this polycotton lavalava
wraparound hibiscus paradise of Pap'toe,'Tara, Otahu—
the happy coin marts, the fly-by-night clearance outlets,
the stack 'em high, sell 'em cheap, plastic whatnot bins.

A pearl nacre overcasts closed abattoirs of Southdown,
colonial headquarters of Hellaby's meat empire,
shunting yards of Otahuhu Railway Workshops.
Two-dollar leis sway outside shops on Great South Road.
There's Fiji-style goat curry and Bollywood on screens,
kava, taro, fish heads on ice, hands of green bananas—
no sign of Sigatoka blight amid tart tangelo pyramids.

The suburban origami of bungalow roofs is folded over,
under the warmth of 'Mangere'/'lazy wind': so hot and slow
it barely moves the washing on thousands of clotheslines.
Planes touch down; sirens yammer through the tail-backs;
Macca's golden arches sweat the small hours,
and a police chopper after midnight bugs the sky;
weaving back and forth over quiet streets of Manurewa.

A Walk Through Albert Park After an All-Night Party

Like an old magnolia's magnificent candelabrum—
flames of white flowers which gutter and go out—
life goes on without us in particular,
without us in earshot of any prayer breakfast.
All is written, in snatches at odd hours,
and sandwiched into centennials, or dawn parades—
like weather turning from sepia to television.
Even twigs have the hooked forms of alphabets,
and fool's gold pours from sunrise's crucible
into fires of electric remembrance.
The lightening trees comb out old petals
to print them on earth in new fonts.

Big City Rush Hour

Cloud pops out,
a body-builder posing.
Heat grills each car on the grid,
bronze light slashes off the windows.
A bus sways forward concertina-style.
A finance house stacks up its cool vertical lines,
calculator-thin.
This town stands as open as an airport lounge.
Everyone looks like a new arrival.

Isthmus

Sugar Town's rush hour fills choke points below
the biggest exclamation mark on death row,
a concrete hypodermic lit by gamble fever,
the watchtower needle struck by weather.
Kite flying in forked lightning, ant trails,
skull headlands whose houses gleam gold teeth:
I nibble at the corners of dark cloud reef.
Woks singed over flames in food halls;
white pelts fur gutters after hail falls.
Forklifts carry pallets, and engines growl;
off hot pavements steam plumes; high heels clatter.
Yellow petals tumble in memorial gardens;
a mānuka bud is a song in the city of sails.
The siren calliope serenades harbour mermaids;
anorexic spectres waver in door plate glass.
Lights, a pimple rash on pinched neck of isthmus:
the container ship glides under blood orange moon.

Summer Catamaran

Tāmaki Makaurau, mangrove-land,
whose waters glug against wharf pilings,
shellback tidelines are your stretchmarks.
Salty city hissing between sea and sea,
I snatch glimpses of your panoramas,
air masses colliding like silky serpents,
thin grey membranes slithering with rain.
Subtropical, left to your own devices,
you set a cluster of arum lily cadenzas
coursing through the morning shimmer,
following the glassy curves of waves,
their luminous green fallings which lilt
to the shadowy beat of dragonish ships.
Heart rocking, the harbor cat takes flight.
Ecstatic, the mouth declares an interest:
to be anchored deep in the foaming drink.
Engines drum their fists to feed us
into the fathoms of the rippling current.
The boat is taking us into her confidence,
showing us the evidence, racing us away,
towards cumulus sailing high over the bay.

King Tide, Northside

The moon is close, at her perigree, imperious,
summoning the salty fever of a king tide.
Volcanoes seem to change position,
to drift further out, or drift closer;
and creeks are frothy-mouthed.
What's salvaged from ocean
might splash up on shore,
ferried from creaking timbers anchored well out,
gilding what it covets with a kia ora tātou,
and a good sousing for whatever can be caught.
Tank Farm to Silo Park, they are keeping
their heads up, though boardwalks are lapped.
Paddlers frolic; sand flaunts its wet silks.
Crowds are shoaling like inanga.
The king tide purls on Meola Reef pathway,
and makes a long grab for East Coast Bays,
The king tide casts a net for gasping creatures,
for reclamation of the waterfront,
for the holy scallop of sand in every blessed cove,
knowing that if you cut a thousand metre channel
between Otahuhu Creek and the Manukau Harbour
you could create Aotearoa's third largest island
to ebb around, searching for wetlands.
And Auckland's flapping like a kahawai,
flapping greeny-blue and silvery,
above all the speckled cockled shelly beaches,
as long-legged girls walk by the creep of the tide,
and the biceps of blokes bulge, hefting a rugby ball.
Pōhutakawa know the king tide well;
they cliff-hang like trapeze artists,
branches parallel to the ground

and demanding elbow room.
They have a ring-side seat.
At night, the old soak of the sea
will go rolling, rolling, rolling home,
dark beneath the phosphorescence of the city.

Between Two Harbours, a Poem for My Father

Portage Road stretches between two harbors.
You are here. Sun's on the face of the deep.
Small green volcanoes rise like tsunami waves.
Clouds darken, rain-slicked, then unreef.
A lizard ladders up a wall. A wing tip turns.
An ant strives along a concrete pavement.
Wind bounces through pinnacles of tall trees.

Dazzled traffic waits at lights in trapped shoals,
stopped by red beneath three-masted clouds
that pass fast as bows of racing schooners.
Windscreen wipers fend off rain-slick blur,
but it swims anyway in my green realm.
Showers skip or slide over hulls of cars.
Sea's an echo sounder for Auckland's shells.

Absolute abba abba, the sun, drowned
into this world, rose, daylight before dark,
to become a ship drawn by the grateful dead,
of whom . . . I swallow this bitter medicine.

Saltwater shawls fall. Tears, spray and foam
curl gold and grey to scud as veils of wet,
running down reflections in corroded chrome.
Wraiths I pursue till sightless with my heart.
Your spirit walked north across the brine—
so home the sailor, the airman home for tea.

With isthmus for compass, skies are clearing,
full-sail blue, like proud regatta clippers.
Dolphins breach in arabesques to tumble

through bubble towers lit up. Dungeon
torches burn with green flames at depth.
Aureoles crown absinthe's sorrow.
From seaweed tangles I woke this morning.

Flying boat engines chatter their reverie.
White terns are wind-swept in accelerando.
In slow formations of gulls that follow,
I trace your wake on echoes of the sea.

Takapuna Beach

A radiant glut of water, a marbled ocean,
luminous like the glittering green heart
of a pounamu carving revolving in the mind.

Aotearoa's a dreamboat on a perfect ocean,
the America's Cup's found in a cornflakes packet,
a runabout carousels loudly round a ruffled yacht.

Daylight's Ferris wheel turns, the ocean burns,
silky tendrils of surf, all gurgle and fizz,
dry out into sand and scrunched shell.

A bounty of boutiques smelling of ocean,
a breeze is stroking the back of Takapuna Beach
disappearing into the sun's gift-wrap of glare.

Flung up above the rim of the ocean into silence,
the evening moon glows orange like barbecue briquettes,
the sea goes on writing summer's outline in foam.

An Apparition of Books

I have a hymn book in a hatbox.
I have a Bible chained to a table.
I have a book that could only have emanated
from a criminal lunatic asylum.
I have a book to bury your bonce in,
and dig it up again,
once the worms have picked it clean,
leaving a grinning skull.
I have a book larded with lunacies
and blasphemous licence—
a book on the Index Expurgatorius,
that to read is a sin against the Holy Ghost.
But a book that remains shut is just a block of wood.
I have a book with a broken spine,
lying face-down on the floor.
I have a book, dog-eared, battered,
pulpy, rained-on, buckled,
that has tumbled along the street.
I have a book with lepidoptera pressed
between the pages.
I have a book with dried poppy juice
nestled lightly in its gutter.
I have a book with chapters stuck together
by the lees of a full-bodied red wine.
I have a book made brittle by the sun,
the ink printed on its paper
barely able to be made out,
even with a magnifying glass.
My multitude of books blossoms like a tree.

Titirangi Considered as Wearable Art

A fringe of heaven, half-clad in glad rags
of mist embroidered with drizzle,
your weatherboard, brick-veneered,
rubber-wheeled, possum-furred build-up
extends from roadways and bike trails,
from mown verges, and from forest arcades
that, mud-stepped, down gullies parade,
as if to salute shops along your main drag.

Bush suburb spiraling, a fern provider,
you're decorated by wasps' paper nests,
and by pole-houses that want to flap out,
like wind-cradled box kites pulled taut,
while birds scatter-wheel to flutter
over canopies of trees, rooted in legends
dug from the skull of the moa, and
hymned in the rasp of the cicada.

Silver sequins tremble on leaf-weave
of shawl draping your shadowy ranges,
and rolling to the lace of Tangaroa's sea.
People of the land carved Tāne from kauri;
sawmill blades set the god free to change;
but he crumbled among moth grubs, breathing
out showers of sawdust in a kind of bleeding
to stain subdivisions that no longer believed.

Titirangi, your sunset blazes in amber resin,
your huia feathers gleam in museum gloom.
Ferns lose themselves; darkness finds coast;

a blurred kingfisher flees from a fence-post.
Eel-ladders descend to the world's womb:
stacked and storied trenches of Hine-nui-te-po,
her kiln-like cave, from where shapes grow,
and the first frond of morning uncurls green.

Atua of Nowhere Zen

Elders photographed staring at gold-rush sun
could not see daylight through a Union Jack,
or rabbit after rabbit bolt from the gun.

Kids in cotton smocks made sing-song;
mustered for Anzac biscuits, gathering
blue-gum leaves to blow a cheery tune on.

Merino jumpers were strung along
the wee gully; with father out fencing,
a slip of a girl tackled the flock alone.

Hail ploughed its block of despond;
thickened a Captain Cooker's hairy back;
encased a sod hut; flattened a fern frond.

The far volcano's catapulted boulder
dropped from dug-up sky like a hot scone
to land smack on Lake Taupo's kisser.

Tuatara crawled to the swimming snow
of bridal veil falls, that had such a glow
as worms had prophesied, under Waitomo;

but hiding out like a bush-ranger's grave is
the spot where all rain forest goes to rack,
and only the caterpillar remembers this.

The historic places turn towards a dream
while necklaces of votive whalebone, worn
by astronauts of inner space, gleam.

Clouds sail sweet bouffant flotillas;
possums stew; sheep cook by the book;
a god-stick spells tales of grandmothers.

The tour guide buzzes, like a fly, stuck
in the marmalade of bitter autumn
varnishing all the hills of Nowhere Zen.

My Inner Aotearoa

My inner Aotearoa is smoky blue-gums
in a corner of the khaki paddock,
a crunching noise underfoot from withered grasses,
          the tarred road bleeding in the sun,
          creek beds shoaling as a dusty river,
          bush decked with trails of clematis flowers.
When I only had gorse in my pockets,
I went in fear of the spiralling arms
of Crab Nebula, somewhere overhead.
Now I escape to stamp the black bubbles
of hot bitumen as if treading grapes,
and run headlong up Breakneck Road.

My inner Aotearoa is a need to brake
to descend the incline,
and I want it steep, steeper, steepest.
          A riddled leaf smites my wet cheek,
          a hailstorm of lies
          is illuminated in a lightning flash.
A glacier shrinks to the size of an ice-cube,
to be crunched, steadily.
But dig deep, deeper, deepest,
throw up topsoil till it rains potatoes.
The magnitude of the extra grunt
resounds, as one more raindrop falls.

My inner Aotearoa is a lake's rise
and fall, land's heartbeat.
The transcendental meaning of flesh
is raised on a bier,

              on a balsawood cross,
              on a barbecue grill,
              on a hospital bed.
Light thickens and sours in the milk bottle,
glugs heavily in the sinkhole,
leading to the place where all sinkholes empty.
So just hold your nose and jump,
into eternal darkness made visible.

Dutch Tulips

Flourishing at dawn,
rank upon rank,
they mass in cadenzas,
and glow like kisses,
embroidering mists
with blushes.
Their petals,
unfurling
from damp earth,
dazzle canals.
Flamboyant carousels,
cosmetics in drizzle,
let them tingle and flash;
let them float and sizzle.
Let them shiver and chime
beneath a dull sky;
day-heralds in turbans,
let them sing as we race by.

Amy Winehouse on St Clair Esplanade

A breezy day on the Esplanade,
where nothing escapes the view,
a kid high on a can of Red Bull,
guys in hoodies puffy as cobras.
Drifting from their wound-down window,
the sob-sister on a squawk box,
—make me go to rehab, but I said no, no, no!

Backflips through an ocean's backyard,
with dipsticks, dropkicks, surf wipe-outs,
salt haze drifting like a filmy drape,
floaty over barren rocks, eroded sand dunes,
flowers yellow as a lick of butter,
yellow as sunshine.

I buy a chocolate ice-cream cone for you.
Smiley faces and stuck-out tongues,
there's e-scooters, shiny shells of cars,
and peeled from a seal-black wetsuit,
the pipe-band drum-major's leg tattoo,
—but I said no, no, no!

Your pointy leather boots clack on concrete,
while hunch-backed scolds of gulls
are moving red-webbed feet to a ska beat,
they're crying out like Amy Winehouse,
—ska, ska, ska! no, no, no!

The evening sky vamps like a lava lamp
of tie-dye kaftan mauves and yellows,
and where's that scamp Amy Winehouse

to echo along with the seagulls,
—ska, ska, ska! no, no, no!

PART TWO

THE SHALLOWS

Soundings

Caught in the ear of the wind,
silence stretches for an instant,
then to summer's racket succumbs:
children shrilling out a need;
a doorbell by hawkers thumbed;
pavements alive with clicking heels;
the cool white noise of news, urgent
to natter and bleed through walls.

Growl of bus, beep of car horn,
construction sites to eavesdrop on;
generations making dissent and din—
whine, groan, roar, moan, hum.
Sounds spelling it out as song:
shivery nuances, rising pitches,
acoustic ripples, transmission glitches,
snap of teeth and bubble-gum pop.

The uphill grunt, the glottal stop,
the hit tune warbled from the shower,
while furthest stars since their birth
have been singing like a lawnmower
on a fine Saturday afternoon,
heard from so far away from earth
it's almost not heard, no more than
than absent hiss on a sonic detector.

Yet we cheer them to their very echo:
sing you singers—the time of singing
is not over yet, so sing, echo on echo.
Sounds of many, call over the bay;

carry me back, they sing to us;
and in the end, all are chosen;
our songs lifted from below,
torn from earth to float away.

Oh, that voice of God technique,
those chords of glory, that grandiose talk,
those notes raised by an orator leaping:
Holy musicola, and do-rag promises,
old hee-haw of the donkey caravan;
or snicker-snacker-snick of barber scissors;
Nazi bellow at the Nuremberg Rally—
a cut-off, chicken-plucking horrid squawk.

For the dolphin language, they say,
has twelve thousand semi-tones;
and there's a magic drone that blesses
those who feel it—have you heard, have you heard?
I have heard monkish choirs, skeletons tap-dancing,
seventy-six trombones, a hurdy-gurdy that swirled,
blood's steady drumbeat, polychromatic cell-phones:
all sounds speaking with the mouth of the world.

Drifting Cone

Under the slowly drifting cone of Taranaki,
when evening stretches out from the mountain,
the black tresses of its rivers wind me to you.
Always I feel the cold fire of your kiss,
that frozen fire that scalds my memory still,
the elixir of your lips where love fixed it,
so that I should taste, like tears in rain,
your distant indifference smouldering to ash.

I remember the scent of ferns you unknotted,
the crystal haze of mist whitely shimmering
on the sea-swell of your bare salty flank,
the mane of night on your shoulders of snow,
and the rare minerals of your eyes that flashed,
your distant indifference smouldering to ash.

Tomorrow

Tomorrow, every now and then, the world might end,
but we will be carrying on.
Tomorrow, the whistle blows for the start of the week,
and that's where you come in.
Tomorrow is poetry in the hully-gully of its making.
Tomorrow is the spice paladin's heated aromas.
Tomorrow is the green waving flag of farm hills.
Tomorrow is petals, proud and bright on magnolias.
Tomorrow, everything goes in the rumpus room:
spillage, abandoned card game, unemptied ashtray,
the sticky whisky glass.

Tomorrow is golden chimes, lighting up the lemon tree.
Tomorrow is wild mountain hail, and snow to sea-level.
Tomorrow, in all the iridescence and bewitching beauty of it.
Tomorrow, I got your back and I wanna hold your hand.
Tomorrow, we go as comrades, arm in arm, through advancing years.
Tomorrow, geology is pressing you to coal, then to rough diamond.
Tomorrow, the world's as blue as an orange.

Tomorrow, the world's going micro.
Tomorrow, each of us is moving backwards,
sweeping the trail clean with a branch.
Tomorrow, see you on the flipside, sistah.
Tomorrow, in drist, the rain will dringle and drumble
to form evanescences, vapours, balms, rinsings.
Tomorrow, more bafflegarb, gobbledegook, bumpf;
more officialese, taradiddles, blatteration.
Tomorrow, never give in, never give in, never, never, never—
in nothing ever give in, except to accede to good sense

and deeds of honour, for the sake of others.
Tomorrow, out of the black: ka awatea, daybreak, ocean gleam,
and ripples, and eels crossing vast waters,
and above them, a mollymawk's glide, tomorrow.

Almost Once

Almost once,
timber combusted then flared;
hot coal spent,
the burnt stick bent its head.

Almost once,
each match charred
in matchbox smoulder;
more dead matches, one red soldier.

Almost once,
brands began to burn;
out jumped the devil,
with endless supplies of gunpowder.

Almost once,
stones struck sparks
for revels of light,
that danced in scarlet and black.

Almost once,
a nimbus vanished,
melted to charcoal and tar;
darkness harvested fire.

Almost once,
a book of maxims lit
with hellish glow,
scorching fingertips.

Almost once,
flames flashed from paper,
fanned to a blaze, whirled as ash,
then sank as a handful of grit.

Moonshine

Welcome evening in, hex the colour blue to rose;
take down clouds; fold them like sheets
from the line; put away the sun;
hang a lantern for the backyard party.

Not a moment too soon, the soaring moon,
the cold and clear-cut face of the moon,
a tossed dollar coin suspended.
The moon beckons with a gold finger.

Harbour moon unveils ripples of the night.
The skylight room shows a pendant half-moon.
Beneath the moon, a flowerchild is rubbing
her long hair with a squeaky balloon.

Breeze snuffles brushed scent of mānuka;
something falls across night's axle;
earth cracks its creaking clay under
fish-hook moon; once in a while, a shooting star.

The man in the moon gathers the stars,
and places them in glass jars;
of things on the wing,
they are the avatars.

On Ice

Strange attractor,
this predator,
as if the polar wind
was to plunge its tongue
down your throat and find
its way into your lungs
to lick all lobes
one by one,
turn them stone.

Home to pure science,
this palace.
Terns stitch its ceiling,
and skua wingbeats lash.
Berg giants
raise anchor for open sea,
amid wave splash,
chandeliers,
all the bling.

Illuminations
of crystal interiors,
mazy glitterings
of reined-in light,
here is the Antarctica
you were looking for,
the place
where nothing
escapes the white.

Scale

Jump from pram, a push-chair, with excitement,
leap off springboard, vault from gymnasium,
chase along, surge away, running strong.

If you see something rising, then help it rise,
shin up a ladder, by handhold and foothold,
climb through branches level after level.

Start from a standstill; be bold in movement,
a dreamer at dawn, a stepper on a treadmill,
a stair-dancer soaring on to the next floor.

Strike out for the peaks, vaulting ascender,
steady at the heels of advancing figures,
tramping before you in zigzag processional

to balconies of cloud above stepped lakes.
Go where creeks tumble, birds spiral below,
and drag of gravity rakes you earthwards.

Ascend over years, to cliff-tops and precipice,
to slips and stumbles, ever-narrowing path,
go slowly up the mountain in closing mist.

Warming

Up here, seagulls float like kites on thermals.
Down there, a car canters like a racehorse
through pasture, towards Aramoana.
The giant wharf cranes of Port Chalmers
stand like steel giraffes in a story book,
and time is reluctant to turn the page.

A fishing boat's wake is carving a V
in the freckled salty skin of the sea,
furrowing its calm green translucence,
until the sun squeezes juice from quarter
of a lemon onto the veiling, foam-white,
dissolved wings of a billion butterflies.
Pick up that foam, pick it up, and drape it
across the dry riverbeds of the skies.

Summer Rain

Spring trees grow collections of wands,
to conjure gently the colour green,
but in summer drum-taps bounce on water
to ease a tension of the skin,
and when summer rain thunders,
then starts to dance, it is itself the romance,
prancing down the street with silvery feet,
kicking a frou-frou cancan from veranda overhang,
splashing the spatterdashes of an entrance.

Rain brings Fred Astaire's tap-tap across the roof,
before a razz of jazz is given tumultuous applause,
the ozone in the air extinguished like snuff
of golden beeswax melted in candles.
Petulant petals quiver in crimson.
Rain bodies forth a spectacular earthworm welcome
from hitherto undistinguished lawn.

After the storm's glance moves on,
silence fills with bird song, the sheen of datura,
sky-blue of the violet, whiteness of carnation,
scarlet glow of Iceland poppies—
until the very nectarines blush, as teeth break skin,
grass dries out, heat splits pods,
and all summer breathes from the garden.

The Shallows

A child pushes out from the shallows,
submerged, then upwards showers
in silver slithering as the pool gleams
its blue eye from suburban immensities.
Lawn-divers, we float and scheme
amongst worms to earth ourselves,
while steering our way between funerals;
and grief counsellors' profundities
about electrocardiograms or seismographs,
like promises of an unknown hereafter,
only lead further down familiar paths
wreathing around the hearts of flowers:
insignificance piled on insignificance,
before magnificence piled on magnificence.

So, we, who had the chance to taste
the afternoon in a water-drop, found
time had become our prison turnkey.
We were held captive by our ordinariness,
while voids searched our fears and chased
us into the deep end of the mind.
We were children under the trees,
breathing in the bouquets of place,
peering into shadows interlaced,
until with slippery blueness we drowned,
and then, blurred with wild glee,
swam up towards the daylight glare,
forever racing the fleeing years,
forever caught by the rush of now.

Three Haiku

Raindrops

Raindrops give puddles
goosebumps, and comb hairs
on a dog's head.

Spider

Parachutist sways
in silk canopy, or sails,
crafty in rigging.

Memory

Potted fern plant
in the curtained room
lives on memory
of sunlight.

Mostly Black

Before, as it was, it was mostly black,
dark beaks, polished talons, feathers, a black
regime drenched in the melancholy black
of rains that took tides further towards black.
From hinges of sunlight hung blocks of black,
and risen humps of islands were matt black.
Cinders sailed from bush burn-offs, carbon black.
Beads on antimacassars gleamed jet black.
Through pine's silent groves possum eyes shone black.
Above tar-seal a melted rainbow turned black.
At disintegration of monolith black,
green, all that blue can be, then back to black.
Green of pounamu lost under lake's black.
Blackout's lickerish taste, blood-pudding black,
and midnight mushrooms gathered from deep black.
Tattoos drawn with bent nib and homemade black.
Batman's mask, a dull sheen of cue ball black.
The primeval redacted, placed in black
trash bags, or else turned out as burnt bone black.
Pull on the wool singlet of shearer's black,
for blacker than black is New Zealand black,
null and void black, ocean black, all black.
In Te Pō's night realm, from Te Kore's black,
under the stars spreads the splendour of black.

The Color White

Fingertip reef,
cumulus ascending,
contoured smoothness of marble statues.

Ocean combers breaking in mist,
swizzles and spills of champagne foam,
beer suds forming moustaches on top lips,
a bride gowned in antique cream tripping
to iced wedding cake resplendent on table linen.

Swoon of midsummer's glare glowing,
fallen frangipani petal stars,
bleached bedsheets hung in the sun,
smiling jackets of porcelain teeth.

Juxtapositions of magnolia and jasmine,
dreamy harmony of blossom,
highest note of a melody in cascades of jazz.

Vanilla sundae, marshmallow, sugarloaf,
meringue beaten into soft peaks,
threads of coconut flesh grated in heaps
like trimmings from a ream,
the arena of paper where these words burn.

When the year turns,
breezes sing lemon and salt of the sea,
and airborne eiderdowns
of dandelion clocks puff along,
like a man whose hair is tufts of cotton wool
floating up into wisps,

sailing in raw cotton tee-shirt, plain cotton pants,
catching the breeze like a seagull feather.

Gusts carry sleet that stings like quartz grit.
Snowflakes flurry their cold socialite kisses.
Morning blows out its cheeks and breathy vapor.

White is the abstract thing,
indistinct thing, luminosity.
Phosphorescent alpine ridges,
fires of constellations in the Milky Way,
crunches underfoot of lace frost,
back catalogues of packed snow,
winter's slippery citadel.

Midnight showrooms of whiteware,
brand spanking new, yet all alone.
Nurse uniform, photo-negative, pigment,
honesty, innocence, candles, incandescence,
soft lamplight, stark bone.

White
white
white
white
white.

Song of the Market Actor

Can we pick up the numbers,
overhaul all front runners?

Can we skip on by the velvet rope,
memorise the right manner?

Can we fool any iris scanner,
grease a tell-tale itchy palm?

Can we unearth sacred ancestors,
rip out the featherbedding?

Can we be ground beneath a guru,
help to ease those growing pains?

Can we trip the wires of persuaders,
reveal mounting inner fire?

Can we behold our franchise options,
slip away the silken bonds?

Can we learn how to last a lifetime,
appear in the final frame?

Can we stay in touch, venture, get more,
push to ultimate levels,

then with a single gesture
blow in to chase down windfall,

roseate through sequinned night,
unforgiving at steel dawn?

Yes, till I take on too much,
toxic loss, your missing funds,
so that then come colder rains
screwing over hoped-for golden years—
in the crash of collateral damage,
love me, love my emotional baggage.

For I am the market actor,
looking for the hidden factor.

The Age of Terror

Praise be to internet, now my mind is a search engine:
a web-headed weave around humanity
every which way that babbles of conformity,
and of dissenters in each departure lounge.
Can you step in the same data stream twice?
Satellites will eavesdrop on your advice.
The red dots dance their moody existence,
chased by cameras trained to turn,
and stealth drones hang in the listless air
listening for heartbeats that say human,
only to hear low hums of server farms,
and the hollow squalls of car alarms;
or is it feedback of prophets alarmed,
walking backwards on peacetime manoeuvres
and humming under flags of convenience,
seen through Google Glass smoked darkly?
But I don't watch enough TV to know,
though Earth's artificial networks grow
to encrypted purpose, so robotic
before screens on-line that fingers data-mine,
putting it down in writing, in lightning;
and then they fold the known universe
into a parallel universe, time out of mind
and back as the peacock's scream
vaults the dream to plume the trees with flame,
while an announcer's toothy grin begs
mediocrity's intense inane: that smile spreads
its chemical haze over Iraq on a rack.
There are unknown knowns, and then there are the drones.
The redacted cell-phone's pixels blink at code black:

you all look alike to me; you fit the description.
We have your signature; you're in our sights.
You are what's cooking on the Cooking Channel,
being waterboarded in sync to the noise
of absolute zero, as if you were Batman
caught in the radar of his own making,
or Gulliver taken in by the Houyhnhnms,
their neighbourly neighing. So, the riot
of gardenias in Pandemonium blazes,
and hearts wilt before tomorrow's sorrow,
and the age of terror is without error.

Methusalem

Shame, a flame-red flush,
the scowling darkness hisses—
thunder-rumble and bolts thrown
to the electric attraction of opposites,
their mutual sickness,
holding a relationship together
with resonant frequencies.
He said, she said, they said, on the salty wind—
salt mines of the crystal field,
text blinking on the blue wand,
that the eye scans.
July's vibrating electro-magnetic field,
oscillating in step, humming in sympathy,
shadowy frequencies joining in,
with infra-dig, ultra-violet, X-ray ring
tones to set up a stone blackout.

In damped under-awnings,
invisible colors revealed,
that ricochet to the bluing of distant hills,
thick vapors on the Waitakere Ranges,
blue butterfly wings almost,
as scales that shimmer sea-green,
and shift on the wing,
gold, sapphire, emerald show-offs,
wing-wavers,
grinding and scattering in mounds, dunes, heaps,
fills, pulled from earth,
discovered, uncovered, chameleon.

We sink into Methusalem and live here,
its resonances,
its lane-bending dreams, grey and colourless,
then blooming with colour,
compounds of lead springing forth
as white-lead weatherboard, red-lead iron,
painting refrangible bullseye Methusalem.
Methusalem, oh yes, its arbitrary
subdivisions
of the sunlit spectrum—
its harmonies of roof-tops,
its bignesses, its hulking monster stingray,
its flounder stuck to mud beds,
its blue deepening to purple,
its indigo and violet bruises,
its blood-letting,
its streets that smack you
in the face with their indifference,
its crowds that sing to many different
notes and chords, its road-hogs.

A clear noise of vehicles and call signs,
mobiles and radios,
sunlight silent in the echo
of post-festival euphoria,
multi-pitched Babel cosmos
of compressed continents through voices
urgent to be heard,
and sunlight falling silent as smog particles
drifting into canyons,
beauteous curves of smoothed-out gullies

running seaward.
The frozen berries sing, and the black bitumen
splits to reveal gravel baby teeth,
the rule of thumb guided along the dotted line,
where they split the atom and peered inside,
logos, eros, budding forth.

The tents of green are gathered here,
in muddied brilliance
of rainbow refractions inside droplets.
The huddles in a darkened care
home are ancient McCahon hills
under brown and black blankets;
and there's white from Moana's necklace;
and white from Rangi's cloak;
and there's red from pohutakawa;
and red from bark and soil—
rust-red, burgundy, russet on the rainbow spectrum,
hazel, chestnut, the ardor of ochre;
and an oily pond, wine-dark, in a glass.

Those moist, cool greens on an Auckland
winter suburban morning,
amid gemstone tail-lights—
the malls that suck up moisture,
and spring it in rainbow-colored arcs
through a plastic straw
between strawberry slush of lips.
Plastic is a shattering of the unity
of sulfur, mercury, chlorophyll, blood,
into separate lotions, elixirs, potions, cordials,

into liniment's spirit blackout in the July city.
Plastic was the future,
in orange, pink, yellow, ultramarine,
in ivory, copper, cinnamon, maroon,
in bright, dark, heavy, light blue,
in fifteen blues,
and so, the color field grew.

Now's the muddied brilliance
of flesh, drapery, water, shelter,
in this fool's paradise of prismatic arcs,
this July city—
clouds a purple-dyed wool piled on benches,
and streaked crimson and vermilion,
smeary as dashed dregs of coffee,
as clotted blood darkly reflected.
The storm closing in, like a border patrol,
with heads of dark rose, foams of dark grape,
a blue-dark pompadour,
fists tattooed by a bruise-dark manifesto.

The blood is sewn together
to float as a fine rain
against high windows and spires,
and above Karangahape,
so see you on the other side
of the underpass, the passing over,
above Karangahape—
its greenish-tinged billboards,
its blue boundaries dissolving.
The blue riders on the storm,

plunging and rearing in foams and sea-salt,
in table-top clutter, in bundles of vegetables,
that are rain-soaked greener-black,
blackened wet by the storm—
its indigo-mania, its sapphire-flash,
its blitz of threads carrying across
azure the blue of the underworld,
the mauve movements of cloudbanks.

Colors running into rainbow darks,
into silver tarnishes and blurs,
into neon's noodle swirls,
into woodgrain vinyl, and painted dirt.
Soakage overwriting blades of grass
with new particulars, with each thing numbered,
with mashing of leaves and barks—
druggists sifting for drugs with a sieve
to strain into reservoirs,
to press out the juices, to knead
the pulp of all the parks,
in midnight shades with vivid blue flashes,
strident hues bleached by headlamps,
a rich umber of landslips for the new day—
and the July city at midnight wobbling
its hundreds and thousands of dots,
like the glow of a forest fire far away.

PART THREE

THE GREAT WAVE

Belief in the Pacific

Yes, night's nowhere, that's where I sleep;
till the sun wakes, stretches, begins to burn,
and greets me when my eyelids, dazzled, leap.

Sunday's hymns laze on ocean's horizon.

Cloud feathers sand white, as green seethes
across taro leaves, across palm fronds' weave;
and coconut trees vault to the blue sky
clang of church bells.

                    A man bows to consult
his Bible; thumbs verse like a hitchhiker,
smooth brow filled with lagoon's light,
though engine drone drowns surf's sigh.

From sleep's hurricane my mind heaves
its woven mats; and I'm this wind-drifter
with fraying map, dreaming of a comeback.

A Report on the Ocean

you want to strip the atoll,
drag it all underwater,
you want to extend your tidal reach,
you want to bring the standing wave ashore,
darker tinge of your deeper waters
lapping from crystal shallows and aquamarine,
where roots of mangrove forests
bend like limbo dancers
beneath flow of warm currents

⌒

you survey, you eddy,
you shuffle, you surround the beach,
you lift the copra freighter
from its rusted anchors,
you drown the taro plantation
in its flooded salt marsh,
islands boggle and settle to your brackish surge,
the niu falls from the coconut tree
and floats out in search of another island

⌒

you leave your message
in anger at the bigger breach,
while buoys and fuel drums swirl
with bottles, toothbrushes, plastic bags,
cigarette lighters, tampon applicators,
plastic six-pack beer can holder
wrapped around muzzle of the dolphin,

driftnets in mazy patterns of screen-savers,
factory trawlers that vacuum shoals of fish
through washes of dead water

⌁

your weather patterns of wild indigo,
your blue starfish, your purple thunderheads,
your forked stabs of lightning,
your hammering rain, teach
and tease in lagoons of your latitudes,
your guano islets lie abandoned,
your powder-white sandbanks glitter,
coral skeleton reefs fall away to the sea floor
from languid lisp of your breakers

⌁

above you, bony ribs of thin clouds hang,
crossed by vapour trail's streak,
planet smudged to high heaven by carbon,
but, colossal from your horizon,
climbs sun, and the frigate bird glides
over the the shining mud, the living crab,
the octopus squeezing through rocks,
the parrotfish that revels in gentle rills
from big waves that undercut
the low-lying road and shrinking beach,
where your tide-beating heart rolls

Between Viti Levu and Tongatapu

Angel wings froth beneath the propellor
as salt foam that surface hysterics mirror.

Edges of cyclones caress
family ancestors in their graves,
and plough beaches like a resurrection.

Time's ascension swims up in shrouds
of bubbles from caverns where seeds grew
years ago, having ripened on mango trees.

Coral grit taps the glass of flash hotels,
their lawns shaded by razor fronds.

Sunset's ripened mango colours rot to
thunderheads dark as rum's demons wrung from
an undertow of clouds soaked by the sea.

Some sharks circle the hull,
white comets diving through green swelling
gardens of suddenly flowering rain.

Brightness

Along the gloss of the coastal shelf
drifts the taste of the ocean breeze,
and a perfume that pours
from trumpets of flowers.
Up there the sky smudges pastel blue,
as the sun's fire flexes
to climb like the flame
of a matchhead held aloft.
All the dancers of the silver meniscus
are streaming and ribboning across
green, glazed transparencies.
Epic fathoms edge their speckled
fingertips into the shallows.
Inside the cloud of the oceanic self,
soaked seeds begin to grow.
A golden comb teases foam against sand,
and the beach is dazzled
to see a sudden clarity begin to burn
through the silken morning,
leaving the world netted in light
that is caught, that is held,
and then drawn tight.

Hotel Pacific

Firewalkers' flames flicker
in the gourds of tourist skulls;
leaf shadows make pillows a chart.
Garlands wear out their welcome;
mosquitoes whine near like Cupid's bad dart.

Dengue fever travels by Fed-Ex jet,
but cargo cult diplomats still flee
the Hotel Pacific slowly.
Lizards cough beneath the floors;
guitars twang from wire-screen doors.

Pink cloud skims the horizon,
beer froth tips on glassy lager.
Viewed from the hotel veranda,
the ocean does crash-dive maneuvers;
blow-flies crawl the grubby louvres.

Chewed cuds of banknotes are flung
where harems of ships' sirens once sung.
Private agents of secret powers
suspend dreams of freedom
for children who gather hibiscus flowers.

Shark-callers feed the fiery furnace
with a chopped-down forest of Jonahs,
and the helix of the tribe twists
between the crests of firewalkers,
until rain starts to fall with a hiss.

Hotel Pacific, washed up in a shopping mall,
trawls into the neon glare of it all.
On the beach a military band
is searching carefully for the lost chord,
as laughter of raindrops snorkels into sand.

The Great Wave

There is no god but God, go mongooses in the monsoon.
The rains thrum on empty biscuit tin drums
to rattle Suva market and flick your face.
The jail's walls are ivory; a rainbow crooks an elbow.
The old shoeshine boy begs for money
for a cup of tea and two pieces of bread.
Everybody wears jogging shoes and sneakers,
the jingle-jangle of the bangle-seller is drowned
by a radio that could walk five hundred miles,
and then go walking on the moon to a bass line by Sting.
A crimson hibiscus lei drapes the punchbowl
at the bar, where I renovate my inner temple
and wait for the night to extend my winning streak,
as hotel staff slice tops off fresh pineapples
to reach garlanded pinnacles of mirrors.
A hinge bends to lift a drift log from the surf.
Thus spake Zarathustra to the fa'afafine:
bruise me with purple shadows of evening fallen
over searched caves of eyes that lids close on.
I listen to the ocean chant words from Rotuma.
The *Mariposa* is a butterfly between islands.
A heatwave, fathoms green, whose light spreads
its coconut oil or ghee or thick candlenut soot,
twinkles like fireflies over plantation gloom,
and heart's surge is the world's deep breath.
I learn to love every move the great wave makes;
it coils you into each silken twist of foam,
blown far, all the way to salt-touched Tonga
with mango pits, wooden baler, shells awash.
My uncle, swimming from New Zealand, wades
out of the sea and wades onshore at Levuka,

where my grandmother is staring out
from her hillside grove of trees waiting for him.

Surge

Noon's blank stare is golden and blinding;
thighs thresh through creaming soda surf;
water's harmonies stream down fluent skin,
lyrical droplets under blue sky's top-spin.
Each wave shapes a loop of crystal ellipse:
slithering lures of oceanic eclipse.
Swimmers crawl currents of the sea,
tracing arcs of immense possibility.
Then a view of the wide moment frozen,
fast shadow stealing in under the ocean.
From deep silence where bubbles boom,
out of the surge, risen from the gloom,
in squiggles and foamy jigsaw puzzle,
thrill of a dorsal fin seeking dazzle.

Moreton Bay

When it's stinking hot at twelve o'clock,
earthy aromas rise and vent.
Something's conjured in a gutbucket
and tossed bloodily in a wok
to quarrel with a guzzle of noodles.
Somewhere, someone faces the chop,
gets the elbow, and, down in the mouth,
thumbs the nose like a clothes peg.
The pineapple factory clanks;
a rock melon's guts ferment,
spilled on grease-trap spikes.
Op shop fabrics swelter.
Crow's caw lays down the law.
Fibrolite freedoms let draughts in.
A tin roof's holed like a colander,
shotgunned with sun's dust.
Shacktown's galvanized-iron creaks
beneath clatter of fangs, claws, beaks.
Pelicans roost on rusty bridge posts.
Moreton Bay fig-trees engage
in elephantine creep.
Against crinkle-eyed seawater,
freckled knuckles row a dinghy out.
Still as a lizard, a man fishes,
at evening for a plume of white stars
to answer the day's long thirst.

Water Views

Piled-up cumulus is gliding to nirvana,
and Dawn has on her bluest dress;
she's always seeking some brighter mandala
over silken banners of hot white sand.
The sea throws down her deepest green,
her surf is hissing like shaken tambourines.

Morning's child reaches to touch water;
sun-pointed deckchairs slope to the future;
in the bobby-dazzle the fizz boats prance.
People paste the seaboard in lashings of lotion,
limbs hug the earth with loving devotion;
through salt spray, with lyrical legs, shapes dance.

Sailors tack seawards on spanked-up yachts,
the sea throws spangles on bright-lit hulls;
the high tide surges with mid-day grace.
Trumpet flowers blare a yellow bossa nova,
sunbathers exist on the promised plateau,
wrinkling to fulfilment through afternoon's space.

The mottled skin of evening is drained of meaning.
Faces squint from verandas to unseen horizons.
A wheelchair lies abandoned by the water's edge.
Shall we rise wise and free from this never-never,
and tumble-turn to torpedo to the far end forever,
under a perfect hemisphere of southern stars?

Steve Irwin Way

The Glasshouse Mountains float on the horizon.
Their strange shapes fill the morning.
They are rum casks rolled down from Bundaberg,
or old pagoda bells unearthed
from a ballasted world of giants.
Steve Irwin Way switches like a croc's tail,
and the shapes vanish as Noosa traffic roars.
Daylight is on slow burn: all grease vapour
and hot air, a sugar fix hitting home.
Reptile eyes surface from cappuccino swamps,
the hills wait to speak with fire's tongue.
Gums sift light and ooze hospital balms,
my sandals feel as slippery as mango skins.
Ironic caws of rooftop crows
sound out noon's scheme of things,
waves of stink ripple through the nose.
Leaves are gnawed into brocade by insects,
bark coffins sewn for their congregations.
High rollers run the sun's lucent comb
over surf shrivelling to freckled foam.
Surfers rise to cumulus peaks and pours
above ghostly jellyfish men-o'-war,
as if to join the white-bellied eagle's soar,
then tumble like pigeons towards an ecstasy,
a rush of bubbles, the laughing buddha of the sea.

Ode to Weary Dunlop

I used to amble, I used to ankle, I'd hopscotch along.
I'd bop, I'd diddly-bop, I'd pad, I'd percolate through the throng.
In the disco, in the bistro, I'd get on shanks' pony,
and traipse it all night long.
And now it's the hesitation waltz, the blind bat foxtrot,
the yearning saunter, the excuse me after dark.
The shamble shanks, the slow bandy legs,
the disconsolate gesture is no walk in the park.
I can no longer yomp across shifting sands
as a riptide tugs quick at my heels,
I'm on the wagon, I'm on the shelf,
I'm looking forward to meals on wheels.
But to tramp and never tire of it,
breathing in jungle's penumbra at dusk,
like that colossus of rutted roads,
that Australian in his slouch hat,
with his remnant of juggernaut army,
that life-saving surgeon in charge
with his wry grin and his sloping brim.
To walk and never tire of it,
as Weary Dunlop never did,
his guidance an airstrip
in the jungle of the mind.
And so I stagger after never-weary Weary,
who had sandals made of old tyres,
and carried that scorched earth smell of War,
drifting our way with the whirring
of propellers and flying boat drone.
There were the Japs, and the other chaps,
up on the screen, with bayonets waved around,

P.O.W. camp barbed wire, David Niven with his frown.
Those feature flicks we watched agog,
before we played it out again on the rifle range
abandoned at the back of the Air Force base,
the sky dead calm with that heat haze,
as men went past in jeeps and sun-baked khaki.
When black and white ran in reverse,
divers burst out of the water backward,
arcing through air onto the springboard
of an amazingly blue swimming pool.
So here's to us now, soft tyres around the waist,
afloat on the vast white sarcophagi of cruise ships,
backpedalling through Asia in the slack season,
looking for the old Burma Railway
and finding the well-paved boulevard.
Things have changed for the better,
gone the forced march, the flogged march,
the sack race march, the dead march,
across an acreage of broken pedestals,
tireless as the ghost of Weary Dunlop,
whose men once shuffled forward
with the sad wallow of tyres gone flat.

In Crematoria

My cyclone unearths a sacred larrikin.
My boom water stagnates in beercan ziggurats.
My book of scribbly gum opens on firebombs.
My mill of ants seethes like a frenzied caliphate.
My cracked glass smokes out a season of arsonists.
My Yellow Monday crackles with payback's clamour.
My blank TV screen, black as celebrity shades,
concentrates its gleams and waits for recognition:
the spontaneous ignition of daytime soaps.
My true horizon dances on blow-torched grasses.
My dry storm bursts out of the slammer,
to swing down like jailbait from a lightning tree.
My scrub explodes on high beams of heat,
white as. Other colours burn to electricity.

Red Dust

On breath of wind,
red dust's imprint.
The percolator brings
a taste of charcoal.

Scorching heat sings.
To walk stirs up
warm eddies of air
as clothes hang lank.

Hibiscuses wither,
a smell of mangroves,
the mud-glazed river.
Stains on concrete—
rust, chocolate, blood.

Above trees are scraps—
thousands of bats.
Out of melon-scented
buttery dark,
barbecue smoke.

Night lightning and
smack of hailstones.
In the downpour,
hordes of cane toads
splash along roads.

Spider Moon

The spider moon burns
reddish-yellow yolky;
sleepwalking through night fields,
a spinner's tranced orb.
Trapezes drift on silk bolas.
Strands carry them a long way
to spokes, sticky spirals,
guyed trapdoors.
Wakefulness in shadows at dawn;
soft, quivering snuffle of a muzzle,
nosing grass and bat urine—
the dog's off the chain.

The bombora of Mount Chincogan
tips a green wave down to the yoga church—
and the amped-up ukulele player
who busks for coins outside the IGA
with 'Yes, We Have No Bananas'.
The check-out chick pops her bubblegum.
Lorikeets squabble beyond the library.
A parrot-man coaxes—
his shoulders are perches.
A galah oohs and aahs.
He feeds the bird clinging to him.
The flock beats wings to a harboring.

Summer kneads trees
the color of a blood-nut hamadryad.
Sunflowers glow more yellow
than fluffy sponge-cake.
Cicadas swing like pendant earrings.
Grasshoppers from fallen clothes pegs leap.
Brush turkeys stalk a picnic sandwich.
Tiny lizards pause, scuttle, pause.
A goanna hotfoots it
over the brickwork of the barbie.
Hot tin roofs
make with their creaking cha-cha.

The air's dry as a dog biscuit.
Stones clang under dusty cars.
The burning tar-seal sports a shiner.
A water dragon's clean-bowled,
spread across the road.
The bat some kid shot at
hangs by claws from a wire.
Birds twitter, rayed out
against the phone transmitter.
The sun's hard-boiled in its shell.
A cloud spinnaker gets the wind up,
and bolts for the wild blue yonder.

Mullumbimby

Frog in a downpipe booms
a didgeridoo croak to welcome
the quick tap and sway of rain.
Another frog calls for calm.
Beetles clap; cicadas screech;
ants jiggle to draggled bird-song.
The sky's antique foxed mirror
breaks into ribboned folds of silver;
each piece falls, a wisp of river.

Rain thrums in tom-tom patter;
tin-roofs drum with fierce run-off.
Windows slam; jasmine snuffs;
day's dim candle-flames splutter;
rooms darken like aquariums.
The town dives, then hangs tight,
a river town, a swimming wraith.
Heartbeats toll rain's listless dole.
Forked lightning jumps. Nerves glow.

The emerald snake of yesterday,
that bobbed its small, cool head,
a green-yellow bead in the heat,
has faded to a motionless grey;
the bootlace suppliant lying doggo,
hid in plain sight on a tree stump,
curled root, delicate in the wet.
Does it sense, through the tree's bole,
old corroborees of Bjundalung?
Nothing moves, except raindrops.

Growth puts out tendrils, then a tongue.
Swaddles dissolve. Rainbows catch fire.
Ponds nurture tadpoles, and murk swirls.
Farm pipes pour pools for lush stalks,
that bud to birth with mud's fertility.
Stippled and mottled amid greens,
a beauteous being flutters divinely,
in reflection from higher creeks.
The snake dances a sacred boundary.

PART FOUR

THE WHALE ROAD

The Navigators

Our outriggers sailed to archipelagoes
    —carrying fish hooks
    —carrying taro seedlings
    —carrying gourds of rain-water.
We navigated
    —by the shapes and colours of clouds
    —by the behaviour of birds
    —by the smell of plants and seaweed.
We steered at night
    —by the moon and stars,
and on the darkest nights
    —by the wind on our faces
    —by the waves under the soles of our feet.
We tacked away
    —from waterspouts
    —from flashes of distant lightning
    —from sleet and ice reaching down from heaven.
We chanted
    —to pumice rafts born in undersea eruptions.
We chanted
    —in storms to oar and to sail-mat.
We chanted
    —through heat-haze to the turtle-sun.

We glided as the frigate-bird glides,
to a rising atoll, until the atoll burst into leaf.
We chanted to Tagaloa, god of the sea,
as Tafola, the whale, breached beside us,
and guided us through the reef,
and then 'ei reached out to lei
in a green garland of islands.

Our hulls sliced across the moana,
weaving together sprinkled islands,
low on the horizon;
awaiting a wave the height of a mountain,
dark blue beyond the reef in primal shimmer;
for life is an ocean wave,
from the creation of the world,
from the time of A'a, te atua, the gods,
from the time of kū'auhau, whakapapa, genealogy.

And now our island soil, torn up,
is flung skywards to hang suspended, trailing roots,
surrounded by empty ocean, vacuumed of fish.
And now we stand on our island,
chest-deep in the ocean, as the levels keep rising.

Moriori Dendroglyphs

green tongues lollop round branches
through wounds in bark with deep
affliction like tattoos freshly fingered

surf's blind gravel spat from the sea
rain streaking a small plane's windscreen
as it lands on wind-flattened paddock

black waves of coal an ancient tide
clenched between clay layers
and just them walking in ideation

on limestone walls under kite claws

Mr Explorer Douglas

Bird cries soar from shore to shore.

You compass islands to hear surf roll.

Above iron pot's steam, ranges writhe.

Blank spaces on charts mark this place.

My watch chain dangles time away.

I take bearings from raptors on the wing.

A kiwi digs with beak walking stick.

What does that rainbowed rain declare?

I was no more than a beetle click,

when I leapt up as a kite rattles,

and fell into my sprawled reflection.

When half of me rotted away, my soul

grew restless and flew to a mountain,

and perched there silent, over carrion.

Maungapohatu, 1916

A black Union Jack flutters in the photograph,
their features swim out towards you.
Light gropes along gullies,
Death's Cenotaph awaits the Last Quake.

The Crown held the land and
vapor trails of Empire wreathed
her blue triumphal arch, which dims now
like the glow from autumn leaves.

Sunk in a polished black dawn, the prophet,
when nails ripped from his yawning house,
felt pushing in from the sea the wind,
smashing up off a skating silver sea.

Black mud slicked handcuffed hands;
his hair was a tangled alphabet.
Horse hooves clacked like skulls;
the barbed-wire harp was strung and would sing.

Explorers

Sunset, and the six billion names of God
written in drops of blood turn to vapour.
We backpack our poems through the bloody flux.
When mourning becomes electrified, whisper
in God's ear, rehearsing the sound of tinnitus,
until God turns His deaf ear, His blind eye.
We call him God the Fibber, God the Food-faddist,
and on and on, mad, madder, maddest.

Baxter's and Butler's footsteps left footnotes
to the Alps which made Buller's gorge rise.
Archimedes could find his fulcrum there,
and seesaw on mountains into the air.
God's own theodolite swings like a pendulum do,
over ropes of butterfat and cow-hoof glue.
Numbers of angels on heads of rusted pins
bless the sugar-bag dears counting their sins.

Forest taken from swamp cracked, then died.
Creaky wooden rooms became hopeful tombs.
Artful constructivists mustered the energy
to bring down from every mountain-side
avalanches of sheep, whales of wool;
their prize rosette pinned to Muttonfat Hill;
their Lord's Prayer engraved on the whisky grain
of black label lakes by winter's bitter rain.

The Backbone Club twists from its own sapwood
a kauri gum bible open to the Holy Word.
Solstice like a poultice draws vapours from land;
Pegasus the Sheep flies with hawk wings in his back.
Bestiaries of butchered birds float down
deconsecrated rivers to the six o'clock swill of town.
Afternoon tea is gilded golden brown.
Fiordland is turning to the deeper dark.

Out of stanzas of turned sod, farms expand.
There sweats a gun shearer; there puffs
a wilderness backpacker; there's Hilary's Everest.
A heading dog barks up Blindman's Bluff.
The quest for an ulterior motive leads us
nowhere but where we were already going,
slouching to the sheep-dip in clouds of unknowing,
God slipping between lattices of neutrinos.

Erewhon Unearthed

Skies run, streaked bloody like fleeces shorn.
Strainers twang symphonies in milk and gold.

Empire Rose and *Sun Boy* sail on the tide.
Daisies nod from spring paddocks, stirred.

Tussock's sunbaked pelt jumps and rolls.
Sugar spoons rattle with tea-shop's prattle.

The moa's calcified rugby ball shines,
plucked from scrums of muddy leg-bones.

Hail pings grave bell-jars in sad chimes;
the snick of tiny hail counts baby teeth,

as tree stumps whiten along Dead Horse Row.
Corsets rip, stripped back to whalebone cages.

Found tremors unearth time's brass-bound capsule.
Wings glow amber inside kauri gum's weight.

Glass arcades surface from submarine depths.
Going for a skate, with beer belly bounce,

truckloads of grey silt are chucked up high.
Cashmere Hills cardigans, faded to pink,

shrink in the wash of a bushwacked laundry.
The smell of money leaves the oily rag,

tossed back and forth by whole earth mechanics.
Coin's flipped downside promotes a fire sale.

Heretics get stuck in with a mixed hot grill.
Bats climb, freed by the great snail's betrayal.

Colonel Shag's cliff-face cormorants preen,
while zephyrs ride, teased by sailboard teens.

The Cloud Forest

In the cloud forest of family trees, with its lineage of millionaires,
dozens of shades of glitter filter down
to the sticky bud of a fern frond,
which is an embryo folded in on itself,
damp brown hairs slicked and combed over into a caul.
It sprouts on the end of a stem, like an Art Nouveau curlicue
in a showroom of Tiffany lamps.
Tribes of glassblowers have lived here, engraving the canopy,
since glass tadpoles first shattered
into Gondwanaland froglets and glacier cocoons were sawn through,
plankton-green, like the interior chrysalis of a capsized iceberg.
Their glassworks blew, molded, and spun pohutakawa nectar
into bush orchids and puffball fungi,
then into vases, bowls and butter-dishes,
and now into hollow emerald fiber-optic cables,
a telecommunications rainforest,
home of the velvet haunting call of the kokako,
place of deep satellite footprints, encircled by white rātā vines.
Silica, soda and limestone melt into a glassware
syrup of foliage,
flowing through the jelly fingers of filmy ferns
in the drizzle season marked fragile.
Unlock the engine's valves, seals and plugs
to let the green goo run free.
Atoms in the molecular structure of glass
soon find their way back to crystalline arrangements,
cooling into branches glazed with honeydew,
into trunks buttressed with footnotes left by generations of botanists
opening a green umbrella in search of the tree genome.
A kākā nest-hole buzzes with cell-phone squawks,
sunlight coins a collection plate's worth of small change,

a logging camp takes root.
The jewelry remnants of depleted forest histories
are placed in scenic reserves—
a settlers' museum of kahikatea butter-boxes,
a florist's shop-window of white kānuka in November.

Turangawaewae

I left my life, held captive by a dream,
and stood in the middle of the Californian
Spanish Mission Revival beachfront,
learning how to build cumulus clouds.
I saw Napier's blue sky pour it on
in the high noon calm of the sabbath,
and become an electro-furnace bolt-on,
whose countrified backwards centrepiece
shone above the tremble of summer's edifice.

Then I trudged the autumn moa-bog,
to honour the Treaty did a hand-jive dodge,
snapping Hau! Hau! salutes at *Britannia*—
a majestic barge bearing Victoria,
though hard to tell she was, from sour
bars of soap, black billy tea, rock flour,
all that candlepower burning pure oxygen
of ideas at Grand Theory Hotel, demolished
after Hell's Gate fires of the last earthquake.

A tui's hesitant song waltzed around
the rainforest silence of bush lawyers,
and love planted flags on icecap pinnacles.
Profiteers through envy and greed careered,
going by feel, their heart muscles pumping.
Rutherford for the atom was still searching,
in a photograph on the milled edge of town.
Tahupōtiki Rātana gave us that winter,
a kumara, a tiki, a gold watch, a huia feather.

In hand-to-hand combat farmers got closer,
leafing through leaves, rolled ever-looser,
until gardens erupted from Vogel's ears,
his beard of spring clematis cut by shears.
As bush began to fill with supermarkets,
as skies began to puddle with vapour trails,
as seas began to poem with stress-marks,
I undid the rusty clasps of an old century,
and stared down into my life turned to dark.

Hundertwasser at Kawakawa

Buried seeds became his kingdom.
A kauri castle, bleeding its resin,
was the amber silence of his tongue,
uprooted to be landlocked fast by grass.
Gold teardrop lakes, encased in glaciers,
dripped him the burning oils of elixirs.
He brushed fragrant orchids sleeping.
He dyed skies grey, then drew the rain-god,
over a magnificent piece of coast drooling.
Inside the eye of brother tuatara,
he saw splintered rainbows of pāua,
and huia flutter from a wealth of ferns.
He bored a hole through rarest earth
to collect core samples of glowing light.
Wearing a necklace of greenest leaves,
he sailed on a tree through night stars.

Len Lye's Wind Wand

Bendy baton, swizzle stick, swagger stick parade,
a pole-vaulter's pole catapulted skyward,
performing spells at breezy dawn;
a spiral inside a clear glass marble,
a twister bearing the bob of a marker buoy.
Within its moist fog coat, the mountain is coy,
the bee rides the daisy flower back and forth.
Tall wand, a dowser's twitcher, down to earth,
curves to the gusts, inclines to the view,
floats with sphere, a bubble on air;
and then conducts an auction tender
between the mountain and the silver sea,
forest and bird, flax and river,
town and country, wave and whisper,
mountain white as Te Whiti's albatross feather.

Trails above Cook Strait

So Farewell Spit, they mocked the seasick;
Tangaroa always gets burnt by the sun.
Bird cries carried by a squall's lick
echo in the ears of Captain Cook,
sunk like an anchor as fathoms break.

Waka creep past wooden islands outrun.
Fish-headed waves snare, skein by skein,
the filigrees of slithery reflection.
Cut those ropes, they said, so the sails can
gather to slowly skywards their way take.

Winged flotillas fly, radiant with lyricism.
Spanked canvas shines in accumulation,
buoyed up by air like honeycombs of foam.
Waves dance in perpetual motion,
stitching the Tasman under swell of moon.

Te Wheke

Eight arms of Wheke connect a sea of islands.
But where does the head of Wheke lie?
Some say at Savai'i, some say at Hawai'i,
some say at Avaiki, some say at Tahiti.
In the strange deep dark where Wheke lives,
his long arms wind and curl far over the seabed.
The drifting mass of Wheke has no fixed shape.
His eight suckered limbs undulate like flames.
He can fit through a gap as wide as his eye.
He can look like a flounder or a sea-snake.
He has no stable texture, but unfurls in patterns.
His three hearts pump blue-green blood.
In an ocean with too many gods to count,
Wheke lives, rich, inky, and many-coloured.
His colours can enfold volcanoes in a mantle,
as Ra-the-sun-god polishes across the moana.
From Nauru to Palau, Tuvalu to Vanuatu,
from Aitutaki to Mururoa, Tongatapu to Rapa Nui,
Wheke, the Giant Pacific Octopus, feels his way.
Above him sails the ancient va'a Mahina-i-te-puna,
with a bow-wave that's flowering into white foam,
and whales are basking in all the anchorages.

The Whale Road

I have seen harpoons glide while whales slept,
but now the whales are surging through,
energy dynamoes in the ocean blue,
Bodhisattvas and protectors, guardians of the sea.
The whales carry the island, the whales carry every island.
follow the way of the whales, the whale road.
Where whales journey, people follow.
We follow the flow of the whales through open ocean,
we follow where the whale road goes.
The whales are wayfinders for our vaka,
the whales are wayfinders for our life-raft,
for our dinghy, for our yacht, for our ferry, for our peace ship,
for our trawler, for our migrant boat, for our cruise ship,
for our container ship, for our oil tanker, for our naval vessel—
and underneath them all, the holy, holy, holy whale swims.
We voyagers drift into the chop, into the azimuth,
into the girdle, into the circle, where all the winds blow.
Step aboard the old gospel ship, the Jonah boat,
with a creak and a shiver away to sea,
the sun has reached its zenith and we must follow—
through the moon mist, loomings, starry darkness,
the holy, holy, holy whale swims underneath them all,
follow the whale's trail, follow the whales,
the whales are surging through.
Om mani padma hum.

Throw Net

Everything spoken whirrs as a wheel.
A fire-truck vibrates in its crabshell.
Surf tumbles storms of white petals.

The yellow flame of the bamboo cane
licks up all the afternoon rain,
to feed the green smoke of its leaves.

The snores of a sleeper on a beach towel
recite genealogy under volcano's glow.
A sunken raft of manta rays stirs after dark.

Hands hula-hula, shaping sandwiches
into islands; mechanically, a shark
takes a bite out of the moonlight.

Someone slings a hammock between trees.
Each wave is a line; each line is breaking;
and even the mountains are setting sail.

The Death of Kapene Kuke

Burning holes of Pele's eyes are witness.
Floating islands glide, planted with slender
and tall trees that are slung with wind-catchers.
A shark hula dances from island to island,
green peaks rise like dorsal fins of sailfish.

Haku Mele the chant-master calls ancestors;
umbilical cords bind us to the earth.
Kapene Kuke the skydiver walks
amongst us, celebrated with flower garlands,
but desecrates tapu when sailors take
rails for firewood and trample temple grounds.

Was Kuke a god? Lono-makua, his rain-keeper?
No, Kuke was not a god; he deceived the people.
Abstracted, careless, Kuke misunderstood all.
At Makahiki, to the thudding of drums,
dawn from its pit of fire is ascending
lighting domains of clouds, currents, blue swells.

Kanaka was beaten by Kuke's sailors, so stole
a boat, then broke it up for nails for fishhooks.
Kuke went to take the paramount chief
hostage. The people stopped him, and Kuke
was clubbed and stabbed. Mother Pele's anger
shone red lava through air, earth and water.

With hiss and crack waves sizzled on hot rock,
as Kuke fell from black lava at Kealakekua Bay.
Pele, goddess of the volcano, turned as cold
as a lei wreath in a United States refrigerator,

and rains stirred, awakening the war god's rhythms.
Kūkaʻilimoku is eater of islands,
swallows them greedily in a shroud of bubbles.

Kuke was washed and wrapped in taro leaves,
then laid in a shallow pit sprinkled with sand,
and a fire burned over his body for ten days.
Freed from flesh, his scorched bones were gathered,
wrapped in kapa cloth and placed in the temple.

Kuke's heart was hung up in a fern hut,
where it was found and devoured by children
who mistook it for the heart of a dog.
Warriors diced for his bones, whittled away
as relics taken for spears and fishhooks,
though some were retrieved by Kuke's sailors,
and consigned to the deep wrapped in canvas.
Kapene Kuke died for the handful of nails
that held a cutter together. Captain
Cook brought capitalism and Adam Smith's saws,
rather than reciprocity and sharing of gifts,
and he was not the great white god Lono,
but one speared through and smoked till flesh seared off,
as the rain dogs ran with the grey rain gods.

Kapene Kuke shot a man who threw a spear,
with his double-barrelled gun, but the man
was wrapped in layers of wet kapa cloth
and so bullet-proof; each musket ball rebounded
and fell, harmless. Then another man struck,

and another, before Kuke tumbled into the sea.
Someone wanted the hallowed slab on which Cook
made his last stand blasted out and taken to America
as Exhibit A; instead, Hawai'i
itself was stolen to become the fiftieth State.

PART FIVE

THE WALL

The Psychopathology of Everyday Life

To be one whose name is writ in icing on a birthday cake,
to be an elaborate baroque curlicue
curving into a marble staircase,
diamanté sunglasses or poolside lounging chair,

to revert to type, to be a stock character, to be a cliché,
to be condemned to the shadows, to a twilight existence,
perpetually re-living the torment of those earlier years,

to be lost in speculation on the Canterbury Plains,
to go into orbit,
to be a flower squashed
by a random footfall in an Edenic garden,

to work loose the wire restraint which is placed
round the head of a champagne bottle preventing
the cork from popping prematurely
in the Bar and Grille,

to siphon off excess anxiety through violent exercise
on the squash court,
to be bathed in streaming stadium light,
to believe in the popular mechanics of auguries, haruspications,
palm-readings, horoscopes and water-diviners' wands,

to be a hairsbreadth away from making contact,
to wade into the surf and be knocked over gently
by the tepid swell,
by a lazily sloping shelf of sea,

to swim to the surface as another cloud-capped
wave swings up and makes a kinetic arc,
gliding smoothly towards the beach before toppling
under its own momentum,

to be a rock-like monument, a human alp,
to be like the last of the deep-sea leviathans,
to identify with an elaborate junk sculpture, cameras
boring in, totem poles of slung, splayed monitors

rising from every side—huge, high-definition screens
playing up exaggerated images of body parts: knees as epics,
armpits as marathons, an eye enclosing an ocean,
a shaved hair follicle singing like a kauri tree stump,

to be alone,
to fall silent.

Is This You?

Clinch, hug, break, smile, raise your hands together.
Fist bump and high five are preferred to middle finger,
but no-one watches the humdinger,
so you move fast and break things,
being fake-happy, and living at
sometime in the mid-Pliocene era,
when the world was a whole lot warmer.
So what if the clinks of dollars ring true—
the rest is tiddlywinks,
and you get no change from nineteen ninety-nine.
Is this you?
The boomtown bombast is moving your way,
to bring winking bracelets,
the feel of yesterday on your skin—
that's the you that's trying to catch
the colour of each season,
the taste of the morning,
the noise of the evening,
the crush of happy hour.
All containers are overboard,
and you're my shipwreck of the dinner set,
on the rocks with a twist of lime.
I got you, but as tunnel vision.
I got the herky-jerky jump-cut you,
The Nouvelle Vague in vogue you,
but count on it—
you will eventually wave and waver
and rise in stardust, whistling,
to where some brand-name bling-meister twinkles.
Dinosaurs will be doing lunch.
That will be something, something to tell your children.

Hang On Soapy

I worry about money; you worry about abusive family.
I'm the weird girl; you are too normal.
He is the adored handsome son who wants a sex change.
She's into self-harm and the beauty of privilege.
I believe in flashbacks; you live only for the future.
Your anxiety attacks precede my bereavements.
Too many bitchy friends make for a bad brew.
Your earrings are cherries on a tree in Otago.
They say everyone feels a bit light-headed,
now that the mall has been spritzed with scent.
She never toppled into the tub of purple,
treading out the soapy grapes of vintage
in jealousy, the jealousy of someone who saw
creative writing students confide in each another.
The endangered frog is green with chlorophyll.
I wish I was just one of the everyday people,
for I am green, too, green to the gills,
yet cushioned from worlds of hurt by you.

Kate Winslet Promotes a Credit Card

She's contorted over script or contract.
She mimes reading with hunched back.
She's somewhere inside *The New Yorker*.
She poses beneath the legend: *My life, my card.*
She sucks, like a straw or claw, at her finger.
She exposes, like that of a great ape, a foot's sole,
wrinkled as a map of the moon.
She has a big toe that seems so much older
than the rest of her, as if she has just
arisen from a bath, and that big toe
was under longest.
She has that toe as the punctum,
so that we must contemplate smoothness
wrinkled in a bath: that wrinkled, sensitive
point of balance exposed; just out of its shoe
and already cooling the blood.
In a photograph the colour of greyish tin,
she feels through the sole's drumskin
each reverberant step of her life.
She's architecture; she's an archive;
she's a firebird; she's a poet's metre,
putting her best foot forward.

After Reading Eleanor Catton's Birnam Wood

Lady Macbeth's roses are bloody
warriors, raised in a vase;
her wine has body,
and is heart-warming red, through and through.
The king in his cardboard burger crown
is feeding half the town dump
with a left-over seagull cull;
his bloodied hands point
this way to the recycling depot,
that way to the trash compactor;
and the bright carbuncles
on the backsides of tin hides of cars
are winking their turns left and right
into the McMansion maze
of Birnam Wood, where each suburban subaltern
in real-estate uniform
readies the trampolines of screens,
as a sudden sob-sister's siren call
ferries another fallen queen
to the ambulance bay of a hospital.

Death Warmed Up

Party, party, party—and amongst them walking, Mister Death.
Understand: he wants to be your bed companion,
But the door only swings one way for Mister Death.
Beneath the sun, Mister Death's a personality cult of none.
Death might parade naked for your delectation;
Camouflaged in articulation: a grinning skeleton.
Brought up in a moral vacuum, Death never says, never.
Death preens from every mirror; grey panthers patrol the border.

Death, a gambler, stalks and skulks, punter to punter.
Death's nightmare in general is a fear of the funeral.
Yet, no matter how fast, Death comes gaining.
Death's hearse rolls up lickety-split; so, you must hop into it.
Some tussle; some holler; some fight; but all at last lie silent and still.
As, by your hand, Darkness leads you, Death keeps faith with Night.

Watching the Detectives

Unnoticed, lie corpses of weasel and magpie;
the feral pig stinks, dressed in mould.
Something killed them, something old.
He punches, kicks, and swears awry
at wigging heads of rams,
batted back by bleating lung;
they bare a yellow fang, raise a cry,
in acrid tang of urine and dung.

A queue quibbles between tills;
the entrance to the tunnel's closed,
but this is no excuse for the mourners
to drop their casket and rush to the hills;
the hills will be a slog from the word go.

A profit and loss prophet leans at a drunken angle,
running off at the mouth in a jingle-jangle;
his drool's caught by the wind factor,
and spun out as a sun-struck web,
like the web a wasp is funnelled into,
where a tiny spider jiggles for joy,
running across the rigging to snare
with more threads the maddened creature.

Spring's stipple of pollen mantles the window,
a gentle detective dusting it for fingerprints,
in a motion soft as slow blowflies that spiral
out of bodies of dead rats on the compost.
Flies graze on cake; the wind murmurs.
There was a death, but now things grow;
voices writhe into life at the wake after the funeral.

Afterlife

I would dig a bigger slice of the roseate
radiance that spins elusive in a pink cloud
beyond my fingertips, but as someone
slips and slides from the ski-slope every day,
headed for the biggest boulder around,
so my immortal soul turns the corkscrew
to an afterlife of booze and cigarettes
with hammered skin and the skull knuckled.
I make promises to the rock of ages,
then break it up to pave the planet.
Your otter skin pelt skims through the glittery
browed sea on a trip beyond me.
I drop like a sparrowhawk on a pigeon,
or spider on wasp, run like a Norway rat
up a limb to a forking dilemma and fall.
I have swum with the green sea turtle,
pondered a Victorian table,
and questioned the biblical fable,
till it reared up and flew back to bite me,
who was unvaccinated and turned rabid.
I raged like a loon against the hideous moon
that glowed like a spoon over a lamp
to bubble tar, and drew up my blood
into a quasar doused with helium;
the resultant explosion lit the stars
and kept me staring into space
just twelve steps below paradise.

Identikit Male

Unpeel from the magazine sample
the latest scratch and sniff.
Cordite, hot metal, khaki, sweat:
the smell of *Body Bag for Men.*
Warehouse warrens of shelves stacked
with bullet-shaped bottles of aftershave:
the man's shaving lotion - *Steel Capital.*
The chemistry of the elusive god particle
ratchets up the ante to a pheromone frenzy:
graven images of the masculine supremacist.
Issue a summons to the stalker within,
offer a season in the house of correction,
order a paternity suit made to measure,
shut him down, give him his place in the sun.

The Hook of Maui

A fanged shank yanks him from open sea.
Silken jellyfish glisten on hot iron-sand.
Mottled green light tattoos a drug-blue gaze.
Stingrays undulate along sunlit nerves.
The road snakes, and cars fishtail in gravel.
His ears are earthenware, glazed by mud.
Gold toetoe rise in hair-triggers from his armpits.
His filaments snarl round a plastic comb.
Police bolt-cutters snag on his tongue stud.
His lungs are stopped with red scoria splinters.
His lips turn black from a summit's pure snows.
His blanket's unbound clay, slid from bedrock.
Night's moths flutter from the cave of his mouth.
He dreams he's woken, wrapped in calm water.

Smoke

A burning wand wafts in plumes to be exhaled
in volcanic rush, smoke erupting from nostrils,
as if out of vents in the earth, only a devil's dream.

Unrepentant, gathered down alleys to blow smoke
each other's way: each cigarette marks time, ground
out like a coffin nail hammered to a coffin lid.

Each is weighty, a stoned idol, smoke issuing
from the mouth as swirls cast forth, containing
curative properties, powers to raise the dead.

Light my fire, give me a puff, and then burn
down the main drag: for the space of a smoke,
he was wheeling his helix towards eternity.

He smoked the Book of Genesis through prison,
page by page, and aimed a forefinger and thumb,
bang, bang, at the guards the length of his days.

He resembled a blackened smokestack city,
gritty of speech, burning tobacco at midnight,
in gardens of pleasure, till old with taste of ashes.

His smile crooked as a broke-down castle, he smoked
at warnings, the blighted gums and teeth on the pack,
his lower inside lip forever tattooed with *Ake! Ake!*

Bouquet of Dead Flowers

Her body was braille, was scent bottles uncorked,
was the music score her breath hummed;
and beyond us the sun was the giggling Buddha,
robed in saffron, licking his finger
to tear months from the calendar.
The days withdrew from us like acupuncture needles
each morning when we woke up,
and slipped from the bedding seeking the promise
of orange juice you could take from the moment.
We sailed through seas of incense smoke together,
tranced by the gorgeous melodies of Indian-thighed summer,
by the gardens of wild poppies which grew all around us,
in the deserted volcanic quarries of the holiday season.
It seemed then that stereo speakers, always vibrating
their bongo heartbeat, busy bees in the calyx of a flower,
were the hypnotic metal portholes of our ship,
drumming its way through stormy passion.
Spiky juju crystals of the silence between us
were needed to calm that billowing passion,
and the dances we went to at night
only stirred it up, as the whole world duckwalked
with us, or were dirty dogs shaking down,
the brand-new leaves in that summer-of-love tree
fluttering on the breeze of yesterday's sound.

Old School Prize

The timekeeper looks at my date stamp,
my damp pages stained brown as spilt tea
or weak coffee, and clocks my bent spine,
the dog-eared corners and wrinkled edges,
the fact that I've been on this back shelf
so long, since some time last century,
would you believe: slim volume, old school prize,
inscribed, beaten-up, dust jacket lost;
and places me in the box for worn-out cast-offs.

The Zero

With a writhe of hands,
this world-famous nobody,
a vacuum really,
an elbow-plucker, one of the fans,
casting about for a way to be felt,
makes a once-in-a-lifetime offer
to become frontrunner;
and this unedited emotional genius,
flirtatious pathological liar,
name-dropper, debt-dodger,
silent taunter, foe,
personal confessor,
wreck on the never-never,
Olympian, winner, game-on
whooper punching air,
this hero ready to go—
is then gone.

Them

They love lie detection tests and detention bracelets.
They inflate a soft toy globe, they puff with notable lips.
They discuss persecution complexes.
They have devastation visited upon them.
They always hark back to analogue times.
They anguish about the good, the bad, the God-bothered.
They make a welter of air kisses.
They demand a simultaneous translation.
They are drifting along a flight corridor.
They are all love charms and spooky coincidences.
They are misanthropes feasting on haunches of antelopes.
They willingly enter a steep weirdness curve.
They seek to buy our love,
and reduce philosophy to a jingle.
They make something out of nothing.
They promise there's a future riding on it.
They want to make this thing fly.
They boost the power of botanicals.
They follow up blood trails with yarrow.
They will take a neo-classical turn if necessary.
They want to lead us through the kissing gate,
towards the big kiss-off and good-bye.

The Wall

Because it's there, Mallory.
These, and all our rough notes, must tell the tale—
that we knocked the bastard off,
then split for Tranquillity Base.
Everywhere the glint of gold,
wonderful things—
but time to pull finger, because more
will mean worse,
and I must get out of these clothes and into a dry ginger ale.
Yes, any colour, so long as it's black.
They are crying all the way to the bank,
they are going to spend, spend, spend.
Damn you, one per-centers:
every other millimetre fool's gold,
at the thirteenth hour on the thirteenth day
of the thirteenth month.
Cast and recast as an angler at the lake of darkness,
leave your caste as one who misspoke, then woke.
Who goes as a joke?
He never kept his promise to build the wall,
greater than the Persian Gulf, the Great Wall of China,
the firewall of the Pentagon, the Berlin Wall,
the wall against Mexico, the West Bank Wall—
a wall the size and weight of Manhattan,
or a trillion dropped dimes.
Holy moolah was falling peacefully,
the TV quietly blinked and bled.
I never get out of bed
for less than the price on my head.
The engine idled and then it roared

with all its horsepower; it wouldn't be ignored.
The leaf blower rocked and rolled
every leaf to its appointed place.
A shower of rebate coupons fell in a field.
The heartland is a target poster drilled with bullets
that tourists fly over,
and the only thing growing is private prisons.
Put a frame around it and put on the orange jumpsuit.
Forget all those imaginary islands
where Havana is smoking like a cigar;
forget all that cross-Pacific longing for packed beaches,
for the roadstead where sailing ships met,
for blue jeans faded as Antarctica sky.
All they ever deliver here
are cardboard boxes full of computer parts,
as if there is nothing outside the computer,
but some boxes, I believe, contain pizza.

Wheelbarrow

Dropping cigar ash,
puffing on a stogie,
Bill Williams groans:
This tastes good to me,
this tastes good to me.
Eyes glazed by whisky,
he wheels onstage
his red wheelbarrow
at the wheelbarrow convention.
On his head,
a white chicken on one leg
spins like a weathervane.
So much depends on the poet's
backwards shuffle exit,
as he intones:
Stay in your lane,
Walt Whitman,
stay in your lane.

PART SIX

BEACON

Distant Ophir

I went looking for the nightingale,
for the rose, and found corrugated iron,
scent of wild thyme, cry of a hawk.

I felt a breeze lift in the orchard,
to waken the leaves from slumber
and entangle memories in apricot heat.

Monday was washday, Tuesday ironing,
Wednesday cleaning, Thursday baking,
Friday shopping, Saturday sports games.

Sunday meant church, promise of roast dinner.
Air stood dry and warm beneath pine trees.
Crickets leapt over sunflower radiance.

Summer's elixirs glistened in green jelly.
Jam was given in peach and cherry.
Quicksilver sank in the foxed mirror.

The breeze, a stir of quiet fingers,
plucked at floury puffs of petals,
fluffed sponge cake, buttered big scones.

Furniture stacked, empty windows blank,
fine bones showing, faded curtains folded,
the farmhouse went for a knockdown price.

If I peer hard now through the late afternoon,
I can almost see as far as distant Ophir,
and cargo from Otago, raising the dust.

Sunday's Song

A tin kettle whistles to the ranges;
dry stalks rustle in quiet field prayer;
bracken spores seed dusk's brown study;
the river pinwheels over its boulders;
stove twigs crackle and race to blaze;
the flame of leaves curls up trembling.
Church bells clang, and sea foam frays;
there's distant stammers of revving engines,
a procession of cars throaty in a cutting,
melody soughing in the windbreak trees,
sheep wandering tracks, bleating alone.
Sunday sings for the soft summer tar;
sings for camellias, fullness of grapes;
sings for geometries of farming fence lines;
sings for the dead in monumental stone;
sings for cloud kites reddened by dusk—
and evening's a hymn, sweet as, sweet as,
carrying its song to streets and to suburbs,
carrying its song to pebbles and hay bales,
carrying its song to crushed metal, smashed glass,
and fading in echoes of the old folks' choir.

Autumn Blast

From a high rostrum conducting tantrums
the wind polishes bluff and counter-bluff,
brings feathery rain to muffle dry leaves,
blows crumbs of cookies from cafe tables,
leans iron grillwork against pitted graves,
and barrels round rusted incinerator drums.

It rattles roofs like quick steeplejacks,
pummels wool beanies, gets under golf caps,
makes business shirts tucked in flap loose;
sly, it cat-licks corners of squinting eyes,
and flows a finger touch over ears across lips,
sibilant as stewed tea sucked between teeth.

To pinged road signs yellow as gorse,
wind sings, to slouching lanky schoolboys,
to earth mothers, too, whose children
running, circle them like gleeful moons,
to powerlines, airstrips, and the see-saw sea
carries its hoarse tune, to farm and to fleece.

At last, the gale croons through the manuka,
which twists and turns and seethes in its roots,
the storm gathering up skerricks of cloud
shadow, like merino yarn dyed deep indigo
and spun into a nightdress that, weighted
with rainfall, is put through the wringer.

River

Begin, spring,
on steep range.
Unfurl fern-scroll,
in light sing,
glance off things,
shimmer by swimmers,
swirl green as willows
stirring tips in summer;
surface under bridges,
while land turns,
to autumn,
where leaves freckle,
winds raise chaff,
dust braids thorns,
hawks hollow the sky;
and warmth creeping
from currents, open
slather for winter
ocean
ever-closer.

Southern Embroidery

A killjoy's claw, a feathered dawn,
the liar's tripwire that traps birdsong;
the kāhu's lunge, a car's speed,
magnetic mountains burning white.
Turquoise lake; skeletal rock clack
to sound the glooms of algal blooms,
freak-out traverse, funky forest floor,
blood-hot springs and hail's cool millions.
A rainbow sifts gravel for color.
Rusty prayer-wheels of seagulls turn.
The whale's maw pulls everything in,
while octopus tentacles with motion seek
sudden fanfares of dolphin whistles.
Sooty shearwater flocks crowd the sky:
drawn black thread, thicker and thicker.
On a single breath float moon and feather.

Fiord Haka

Rūaumoko slaps thighs, thumps
torso, and groans heavily,
busting moves to rattle gravity,
needle-scratching a seismograph,
making dolphins leap for the starry.
Our echoing ship rumbles, bumps,
and the fiord wobbles up from sleep,
whaleback thrashing around midnight,
before gurgling back down to slumber,
between rockfall splashing hemmed.
By day's steepled buttresses we tramp,
next to river's muscle-tug flow west,
rain a velvet-nosed champagne wetness—
such fine balances of skimmed rainfall,
such varieties of mould and mosses,
on pathway's crumbled clay crust
a dolphining fern curve, a feather flutter;
while in haphazard winks and touches
broken sunlight brightens the gemmed
webbings of branches, water's drift,
all misty impediments to a clarity
difficult to determine in unsettlement.

Beacon

The glow-worm says, let there be light.
Axes bold as love strike for the heartwood.
The kauri table remembers the forest,
and the conch shell calls to the sea.
Through a candy shimmer the waves
on shore open their summer novels.
Crickets' midday curriculum goes scritch-scritch.
Kazoos, comb-and-paper, and harmonica
begin the bee and wasp summer orchestra.
An orchestration of herds, too, undulant
as tentacles and flowing like a lowing river.
Stones rattle backwards at Trotters Gorge.
Lake salmon leap in silver-blue plumage.
Four-wheel vortex, chipmunk techno, bleeps at sunset.
A possum growls, another howls, a third coughs.
Fugitive shadows steal across the moon.
Pebble-mouthed creeks lisp wicked to night stars.
Emerson's *Bookbinder*, cold as an eel's nose.

Snow at 2 a.m.

Hazard leads the way, blossoming ahead,
to the moment grace tilts towards sublime
snow's slow dance on night-time's stage.

Three Japanese students run out in just
white underwear from the backpacker lodge,
brocades of ice sifting through their giggles.

Quantum sky-burial, abstract and bright
mystery practicing the art of concealment,
snow's ghost ships, shrouded, sailing into dark.

Then an empty, green-lighted, silent street,
crystal interiors of freezers on surfaces of cars,
the clear sky alive with shooting stars.

Lighting Up in a Singer Vogue

Winter tilting creaks and groans,
while daylight's hours are buried.
A mechanical digger has gouged
an echo-chamber to pipe seagull cries.
Wrung breeze by breeze, soul rolls thin.
Surf streamers flex savage wave crests,
under a sky of white albatross wings
launched for the blurred arc of ocean.
Mist is flying like pages torn from books.
Slid beneath a sparse quilt of snow,
land's skeleton reaches to hug you.

Postcard

Opening a refrigerator,
you find Port Chalmers.
Now and then a little light comes on.
Two bottles of milk gripped like white breasts
in the fists of a milkman.
In the dairy,
a member of the counter-culture grinds the Turkish blend.
A fly reads the fine print on a fishtail.
Rain is a sad lover,
chucking cheap beads onto the cemetery grass.
Sparrows disco dance in the trees above.
The wind vacuums the flash Wool Board carpet of the sea.
Later, the sunlight tenderly bandages a wounded look.

Drift North

In Oamaru in early Spring,
marking the Day of the Dead with a sundial,
you can face the cemetery from any direction,
and still drift north.

You quietly take your place on the bush trek,
to begin at the start of the day,
where a sandwich cutting leads to the road,
for the drift north.

Bus stragglers muster at the terminus,
wool-gatherers wait in line with knitting,
the backpacker's waving single-handed,
on the drift north.

Tusker, an up and under speculator,
comes a gutser in a puggy paddock;
a grubber, a bit of a biff, then a try,
next the drift north.

Shunt to Parnassus, happy as Larry,
lashed to the wheel in a tangle of weather,
doing the ton in a lather of leather,
just the drift north.

In Kaikoura, you take a squizz,
at waka wake or whale spout-fizz,
while the sky dribbles sweet nothings,
a spindrift north.

The earth embracing kith and kin,
nearer by far to what is at a remove,
traces elements of blood and bone,
seeks the drift north.

Lights fail, snow turns to hail, fences run along,
pets scoot, possums cough, pigeons pack a sad;
trees split, angels flit, mountains winch on by:
it's the drift north.

Mount John Observatory

Drams of dew shove stars out at dawn.
Dreams of wilding pines stalk tussock fog.
Mountain gowns in pristine satin fold
alcove upon alcove away, to await storms.
Creek music mutters from fiddlehead ferns.
Bees zap lupins; glacier grins at glacier.
Scrubbed-clean scenery hangs its calendar
of lakes at a point in space
where sky's blue crush begins.
The stone sails beneath the sun.

Desirous of mud, of sacks of spuds,
of cows in ranging crowds,
and un-coffined by tumbled outcrops,
earth rises from the roll of scree slopes,
hauls through dry bush in stillness,
feels dusty tyres in revolution,
their makeshift patterns over distance,
then runs on under falling night, satellites,
moons of Saturn seen through a telescope,
dark's singular tumulus of Mount John.

Quake, 22nd February

Clocked at nine to one, the city rocked—
then, un-Christchurched, jumped and bounced in
the strongest ever recorded up and down quake.
Plasterwork was a child's plate of jelly dropped.
Through fissures wide as a street, spirit figures slipped;
and rivers whipped their gravel braids.
The old raupō swamp sagged like a trampoline.
Asylums crumbled; a time capsule popped.

God's finger moved, and having moved broke off,
to roll away into quick-sands of risen silt.
A scattering wall of bricks fell across the sky;
and clay slapped to make a golem shrank away.
A chess knight rode across a fever-white grid.
Keys to the Absolute unlocked doors to a Void.
Earthquakeville was a dungeon, damply out of joint;
all the toads escaped, scattering boulders as they went.

Sinkholes rappelled through geological time;
Four Avenues was a broken Harlequin, nursed by Columbine.
Dust whisked about, like grimy Victorian skirts;
soapbox orators of Cathedral Square fled their desserts.
The Strip stripped down to the Avon; the Avon sailed to sea.
Town bells failed to clang with hour-keeping urgency.
Just below the surface, making the surface ping,
a swamp fetus was fluttering, fluttering like a gauzy wing.

The Plastisphere

Ocean's on a bender, it's a hot tub ocean,
gulping chemicals, scavenging microplastics,
chest-deep in sea-wasps, pink sacs of box-jellies.
How drastic is plastic now? Confetti afloat,
it's fallen like coloured rain made from nurdles,
bait nets, gill nets, shrimp nets, trawl nets,
polyurethane and nylon bits that swim for it.

Each coast washes up plastic souvenirs,
that may, while broken, last a hundred years.
A single-use plastic planet's cling-wrapped;
forever residues in the deep marine crumble,
with nowhere to flush away those flakes,
that circulate in trillions, vaster than empires;
the unfurling surf laden with apocalypse.

Crab Nebula glows with the fiery filaments
of a supernova from a millennium ago.
Ammonite heads are buried deep in sand.
Gas fields flare on the Taranaki coast:
Kapuni, Māui, Pohukura, Kupe.
Vistas of cities on web-cams glow like jewels.
We stare at stars that represent ancestors ablaze.

Ode to the Beach-Wrecked Petrel

Claws grip in gnarled rookeries.
I am brother to tuatara,
a companion to ruru.
I see a kārearea rising at russet dawn
and applaud; I draw breath
at bees in yellow forest,
bark syrups nuzzled
between black chasms of sea
and white chasms of mountain;
at the glacier's goofy foot blue with cold
that slides over rocks, surfing on;
at those bevies of alpine beauties,
shimmery in sunlight with a forbidding air;
at bladdery kelp, bright green as gherkins,
cast up from under brine, bursting with salt;
and at a petrel,
getting the red-carpet treatment
from fallen stamens,
under twisting rātā boughs.

Raukura

Stone clacks on stone,
so, creek lizards slither;
runnels slip through claws,
each cloud's a silver feather.
Mountains flex then soar;
the red tussock pulses.
River's mouth is drowned,
when ocean surges, green
below dark vaulted forest.
The salt spray mist, violet,
granular as dust, climbs
to grasp snow mountains
in fog layers, and above
glides the boat of the moon.

Otago Eight Bells

The fetch of the swell
is pitched up on the beach
to creak of canvas, splash of oar,
while my rockabilly gait along the shore
is like that of some sailor or Captain Ahab
who rocks a peg-leg made of whale-bone.
With quivery wings daylight dances,
embroidered on lacy mist and rosy rain.
White dross drifts and coats
the cross-trees of yachts riding at anchor.
Mist cools summer's festive bouquet.
You might quench your thirst
with a quelled rainshower
grabbed in streaming handfuls
from a hill's wet scarves
of draggled blue delphiniums.
The chill toll of an iron tongue
is calling eight bells
in the mournful wake
of a foghorn out on the harbour,
and something's sailing south,
towards the big swells, said to be higher
than a carpark before
it is pancaked in an earthquake.

Moa in the Matukituki Valley

Moa's a strange bird, old and out of time,
driven from the bush by the Main Trunk Line.
The world is divided between Moa and the rest.

Mountains crouch like tigers, resentful,
and Moa's seeking eyes grow blind,
upstream, wading towards the taniwha.

Moa, you are not valued much in Pig Island,
though it admires your walking parody,
and poor saps poeming to the trees imitate your malady.

Moa's a good keen citizen, very earnestly digging
in puggy clay at the bottom of the garden for a worm.
Moa cracked a word to get at the inside.

Here come the clouds, Moa, puffy like breasts of birds.
Blue's the word for the feeling, Moa, as you levitate,
homing in on living here with your little flock of sheep.

But, Moa, if you feel you need success,
and long for a good address, don't anchor here
in Pig Island, take a ticket for Megalopolis.

Moa's solitude: pacing along an empty beach,
creating in his head a plan to get at the wild honey.
Door flaps open like a wing, Moa enters without knocking.

Not understood, Moa moves along asunder,
losing the path as the daylight creeps
with shadows of departure. Distance looks Moa's way.

Now Moa's there, stoutly bringing up the rear.
Brothers, we who live in darkness, sings Harry,
let us kill Moa, push him off.

Beware the Masters of Pig Island, Moa,
and skedaddle for it from Skull Hill:
they'd make if they could a bike seat of your beak.

Upon the upland range stride easy, Moa;
surrender to the sky your squawk of anger,
and at the gates of the underworld, pass in peace.

With Woven Mats

With woven mats
my muse's bedroom
is an albatross nest,
where she contemplates
the moons of her nails.

Shared Light

Let the light in, let light in—
kerosene light, ice light, coal light.
Light upwelling,
light dispelling,
sparks of light, jars of light,
dust motes swirling in delight.

Glad the light
that comes through night,
shedding light on inner gloom—
rose light, true light, lamp light:
storm lantern burning bright.

Shack's nail-hole light is slight.
And just a zither of light
runs through the fight
of entangled, wild trees;
just a glimmer of light,
down from tree height,
ticks and tocks,
rocking in the breeze.

Ladder of light that leans upright;
river of light that flows from sight:
you let the light in, let light in,
shed light, river light, earth light;
brilliant light to journey by.

Glossary

A'a: the name of an ancient Polynesian god

Ake! Ake!: Māori for eternally, everlastingly, as long as it takes

Aotearoa: Māori name for New Zealand's archipelago of islands

Aramoana: small coastal settlement at the entrance to Otago harbour

atua: Polynesian term for gods or spirits

Avaiki: in Cook Islands Māori, underworld, or place of origin

Baxter: James K. Baxter, (1926 – 1972), one of New Zealand's best-known poets.

Buller: Sir Walter Lawry Buller (1838 – 1906), a dominant figure in New Zealand ornithology. His classic book, *A History of the Birds of New Zealand*, was first published in 1873.

Butler: Samuel Butler (1835 – 1902), a British novelist and critic, best known for *Erewhon,* a satirical utopian novel. *Erewhon* is partly based on Butler's own experiences in New Zealand, where, as a young man, he worked as a sheep farmer.

biff: slang for a confrontation involving an exchange of punches

Bjundalung: Indigenous tribe of Australia

Captain Cooker: slang for wild pig; pigs were introduced to New Zealand in the late eighteenth century by the explorer Captain Cook and soon went feral, disrupting farm harvests

Cashmere Hills: a Christchurch suburb that was largely undamaged during the massive earthquake that struck the city of Christchurch on 12.51 p.m. on Tuesday 22 February 2011, killing 185 people and injuring several thousand

corroboree: Indigenous tribal gathering

'ei: flower garland, or lei, in Cook Islands Māori

Emerson's: a New Zealand craft beer brewery

fa'afafine: Samoan term for transgender or third gender (literally, in the manner of a woman)

fale: Samoan-style building or architecture

grubber: a style of kicking the ball in rugby matches to achieve an advantage

gutser: slang for a heavy fall or a collision

haka: a Māori dance or display; a customary way to welcome visiting tribes, but it also served to invigorate warriors as they headed into battle

Hau! Hau!: battle-cry uttered by members of the Hauhau movement founded in Taranaki in 1862 by Te Ua Haumēne to resist Pākehā, or European, confiscation of Māori land

huia: extinct species of wattlebird, prized by Māori for its feathers

Hundertwasser: Austrian artist Friedensreich Hundertwasser, who settled in New Zealand

inanga: whitebait, or juvenile stage of the fish family Galaxiidae

ka awatea: dawn, daybreak

kāhu: harrier hawk

kahikatea: is a New Zealand softwood found in wet lowland forests; and it once grew widely in swamps and river flats, until these were cleared for farmland

kākā: large, forest-dwelling parrots that are found on all three main islands of New Zealand and on several offshore islands; much reduced in range and abundance due to forest clearance and predation by introduced mammals

kānuka: similar to mānuka but a different plant; in its typical form it can grow into a tree up to 30 m tall; the flowers of this species are usually solitary but occur in clusters; kānuka is endemic to New Zealand

Kapene Kuke: Hawaiian translation of the name Captain Cook

karakia: Māori for prayer, incantation

Karangahape: name of a major Auckland street known for its diverse cultural, artistic and vibrant atmosphere, as well as being Auckland's main LGBTQ+ district

kārearea: New Zealand falcon

Kawakawa: a small town in the Bay of Islands area of new Zealand

kia ora tātou: Māori for greetings to all; hello everyone

kauri: tree much-prized for its timber, and an important part of the New Zealand rain-forest ecosystem

kū'auhau: Hawaiian word for genealogy

kumara: sweet potato

Len Lye: New Zealand Modernist artist known for his experimental films and kinetic sculpture

Levuka: small port town on the Fijian island of Ovalau

Main Trunk Line: New Zealand's main railway line, connecting major towns

Maui: a boy's name of Hawaiian and Māori origin. This name belongs to a trickster god in Polynesian mythology, and was also given to one of the Hawaiian islands.

manaia: mythological messenger or angel-like figure; guardian of earth, sea and sky; a common Māori carving motif

Māngere: a south Auckland suburb

mānuka: a tree with sweet-smelling leaves that can be used to make tea, while bees use its flowers to produce a special kind of honey

Maungapohatu, 1916: Maungapohatu is a Māori settlement located in a remote area of the Urewera region in New Zealand. It was founded by the Māori leader Rua Kenana. In 1916, Rua was arrested by a large group of armed police and charged with sedition for his opposition to Māori conscription in the First World War. Rua's son Toko and his friend Te Maipi were killed during an exchange of gunfire. Rua was sentenced to two years in prison.

Mister Explorer Douglas: Scottish-born Charlie Douglas was one of the great early European explorers of New Zealand. From 1867 to 1916 he recorded the geography and topography of remote South Westland.

moana: Polynesian word for ocean

moa: extinct large flightless bird formerly endemic to New Zealand

moa-bog: swampland containing the bones of the extinct large bird, the moa

Moriori: Māori Polynesians who emigrated to the Chatham Islands from mainland New Zealand around 500 years ago; Moriori dendroglyphs are mysterious tree carvings found only on the Chatham Islands

'nesian: conversational abbreviation of the word Polynesian

Oamaru: a town in north Otago noted for its carved limestone building facades

Otahu: conversational abbreviation of Otahuhu, a south Auckland suburb

pāua: the Māori word for abalone, also prized in New Zealand for its irides-cent inner shell

pack a sad: New Zealand slang for crying or sobbing, or becoming sullen

Pap'toe: conversational abbreviation of Papatoetoe, a south Auckland suburb

Pele: Hawaiian goddess of volcanoes and fire and the creator of the Hawaiian Islands

pōhutakawa: a coastal tree with distinctive crimson flowers and leaves with silver undersides (the name of the tree derives from the Māori phrase 'splashed with sea-spray')

Pig Island: a colonial slang term for New Zealand, because of the numbers of feral pigs

pounamu: greenstone, jade

rata: coastal tree, often gnarled or twisted, and related to pōhutakawa; or a type of climbing vine

raukura: an arrangement or plume of white feathers, traditionally worn as adornment by Māori

raupō: bullrush, or swamp reed

Rotuma: Rotuma Island, the only permanently inhabited and the largest of all the islands in the remote Rotuma group of islands; it is home to a unique Polynesian indigenous ethnic community, and was incorporated into the nation of Fiji in British colonial times

Ruaumoko: the Māori god of earthquakes, volcanoes and seasons

Rutherford: Ernest Rutherford (1871 – 1937), a New Zealand physicist who was a pioneering researcher in both atomic and nuclear physics

ruru: New Zealand owl

Tahupōtiki Rātana: the early twentieth century founder and leader of a Māori religious movement which, in the late 1920s, also became a major political movement

Tāmaki Makaurau: the Māori name for the city of Auckland

Tāne: in Māori mythology the god of forests and birds

taniwha: mythological water spirit, monster, dangerous water creature

'Tara: a conversational abbreviation of the south Auckland suburb named Ōtara

Taranaki: Mount Taranaki, the name of the large dormant volcano which dominates the landscape of the coastal region also known as Taranaki

taro: tropical plant harvested throughout Polynesia for its edible tubers; it is imported to New Zealand where the climate is too cold for cultivation

Te Kore: the Void, the Great Nothingness, in Māori creation myths

Te Pō: the realm of Darkness, of Perpetual Night, in Māori creation myths

Te Whiti: nineteenth century Māori spiritual leader and pacifist founder of the village of Parihaka, in New Zealand's Taranaki region

Te Wheke: giant octopus in Māori mythology

tiki: a carved image, as of a god or ancestor, sometimes worn as a pendant around the neck.

Tongatapu: the largest island of the Tonga group of islands

try: a way of scoring points in rugby union football, by grounding the ball over the score-line

tuatara: a rare reptile found only in New Zealand, that dates from the time of the dinosaurs

tui: a bird native to New Zealand belonging to the honeyeater family; they feed on mainly nectar from flowers of native plants

turangawaewae: a place to stand; foundation; home; a place in the world.

va'a: a word in Samoan, Hawaiian and Tahitian meaning boat, canoe or ship

Viti Levu: the largest island of the Fiji group of islands

Vogel: Influential nineteenth century journalist, businessman and politician Julius Vogel, who was twice Prime Minister of New Zealand

Waitomo: an area known for its deep caves

waka: traditional Māori canoe of varying sizes, including double-hulled ocean-going canoes powered by sails

Weary Dunlop: (1907 – 1993), an Australian surgeon who was renowned for his leadership while being held prisoner by the Japanese during the Second World War

Biographical Note

David Eggleton has published eleven poetry collections as well as several chapbooks and a number of other books. A poet, writer, critic, and performer, he has also released recordings of his poetry set to music by a variety of musicians and composers. He is the former editor of New Zealand's leading literary journal, *Landfall*, and the current editor of *Landfall Review Online*. His poetry collection, *The Conch Trumpet*, won the Ockham New Zealand Book Award for Poetry in 2016. Also in 2016, he received the Prime Minister's Award for Literary Achievement in Poetry. In 2018, he held the Fulbright-Creative New Zealand Pacific Writer's Residency at the University of Hawaii. He was the official New Zealand Poet Laureate from August 2019 to August 2022.